T0078000

PRISON
EYES

LOVE FOREVER; SINCERELY YOURS

authorHOUSE®

AuthorHouse™
1663 Liberty Drive
Bloomington, IN 47403
www.authorhouse.com
Phone: 833-262-8899

Published by AuthorHouse 06/29/2022

ISBN: 978-1-6655-6395-6 (sc)
ISBN: 978-1-6655-6396-3 (e)

CONTENTS

ACKNOWLEDGEMENTS

Let me first give all thanks and honor and praises to my Lord and savour Jesus Christ who has bless my mind to write this book. I would have never thought of written a book had it not been for the Lord. The Lord put this book on my heart to write to many people showing them in my book of how sin can destroy your life if you allow it. But thanks be to the Lord Jesus Christ who sent his word to help us from such destruction. I no longer choose a path of sin. To all my readers, understand that it's dangerous to live in sin. I have tried that life style. It want work because sin is only for a season. The Lord hate sin and he will fight against sin if you allow sin into your life. Jesus said in PSALM 5:5 The foolish shall not stand in thy sight thou hatest all workers of iniquity (sin). I greatly fear the Lord and hate sin because I know what sin has done to my life. So I say to all my readers, pay close attention as you read this book and see how sin has burden and almost destroyed my life. I would also like to give thanks to my mother (*"Sincerely yours"*) who has been with me from day one even when my dad walked out of my life from the time that I was born. I would like to give special thanks to all my Christian brothers and daughter who never gave up on her dad. Thank you guys greatly for your encouragement and your help in motivating me to continue this book, I love you all! May God Bless!

HABAKKUK 2:2

And the Lord answered me,
and said, write the vision, and
make it plain upon tables, that he
may run that readeth it

GREATER THAN ME

This pain I suffer is greater than me
was it my fault or was it meant to be

My heart cries daily, because I want to see,
my love one's standing right next to me

Is it wrong or is it right, to have love
for someone that's out of sight.

A broken heart feels defeated, shaken by the
troubles of the world, do you believe it?

So much to see, no love for me
crushed in pain, surrounded in rain
It's not hard to see
how could this be

These things are greater than me.

CHAPTER 1

THE BROKEN VOWS

The summer of 2003

Praise the Lord! thank you Jesus! you are a wonderful God!.
Those are the words that could be heard from so many people as Kim and
I got closer to the Church. The spirit of the Lord was having a powerful
movement with he's people. Kim is a light skin, young woman and very
beautiful. She was at the age of twenty years old. I was twenty three, dark
brown. I was one of those guys you could say that the party didn't start
until I got there. I had known Kim for two years before we started going
to Church together. Kim had moved in the neighborhood where my
mother lived in Pensacola Florida, where I first meet her across the street
from my mother house. Doing those two years of knowing each other and
spending time with each other off and on. Kim and I was living a sinful
life style. We would party, have sex, do drugs with no care of life and with
no thought of tomorrow.

One day I was visiting my mother before heading to Church. I walked
across the street to where Kim lived with her mother. I knocked on the
door. Kim looked out the window and I ask her would she like to go to
church with me. Kim said, "I'm not sure. I had a long night and didn't
get much sleep. I just came back from the hotel with this guy. We been
up all night popping pills. Let me think about it." Kim said. She left the
window and came back in a few seconds and said, "Give me ten or fifteen
minutes and I'll be ready."

While I was waiting for Kim to get dress for church.

I thought about how living in a sinful life style hasn't gotten me anywhere and how badly I wanted a change. I had been going to this church for a month before asking Kim to go with me to the house of to go to the house of the Lord. As Kim came out the house and we entered her car. I talk to Kim about how badly I wanted to change. Kim also wanted to live a better life because she said that partying every night wasn't taking her anywhere, she wanted better. Pulling away from Kim's place, fifteen minutes later we was at the church. As we exited the car and walked closer to the doors of the church, we could hear shouts and praises to the Lord and we could also hear the man of god preaching the word of God who goes by the name of Prophet. The Spirit of God was moving in a powerful way. Ten seconds later after entering the house of the Lord. Kim was moved by the Spirit of God like never before as though she was having a seizure, many other people was moving in that form and praising the Lord and crying out to God at the same time. The moment that Kim was being moved by the holy Spirit, I ran toward her to make sure that she didn't hit her head on anything such as the church chairs, the wall or other people that was being slayed in the Spirit of the Lord. As I grabbed and held her to be sure that she didn't get hurt. The holy Spirit moved in a mighty way. The movement was so powerful and strong that she was thrown from my arms and hands, her whole body was in the air for a second or two. I grab Kim once again until she had calm down from the shaking of the movement of the holy Spirit. I place Kim in a seat and helped other people to their seat's as well. They were calming down from the movement of the holy Spirit.

As the church service was coming to a closing. The Prophet said a few uplifting words of faith and then went into prayer and also ask anyone who is willing would they like to receive the Lord Jesus Christ as their Lord and savour. Many people prayed the prayer for salvation, confessing their sins and asking for forgiveness and asking the Lord to come into their hearts as the scripture stated from the bible which is the word of the Lord in the book of ROMANS Chapter 10 9 That if thou shalt confess with thy mouth the Lord Jesus, and shalt believe in thine heart that God hath raised him from the dead, thou shalt be saved. I had received salvation when I was eleven years old at a Pentecostal church but as I grew older I kind of strayed away from the church and the faith and begin to get into worldly things. When the service came to a close. Many people of the church begin to fellowship with one another and talk about the goodness of the Lord. Many people also waited in line at the office door where you could have a private conversation with the Prophet. While the fellowshipping was going on in the church. I walked over to where Kim was standing and greeted the people in the church that she was talking too. As others passed by to greet me and Kim, most of the people thought that Kim and I was sister and brother. Kim was so excited about what the people were saying and that made her smile.

I ask Kim was she ready to go and, she said, "Let's stand in line and talk to the Prophet before we leave." So I said, "Okay" and waited with her in the line as more people passed by that was leaving as they greeted us and left the church. While I waited in line. I was so happy for Kim being touch by the holy Spirit. She looked like a new person. You could see the glow of happiness and peace in her eyes as though the weight that she was carrying has been removed from her. Truly I felt blessed to see Kim like that. I also felt the weight removed from her heart that was so heavy with sin. I was standing beside Kim in line to talk with the Prophet. As Kim entered the Prophet private office. The man of god also saw me standing with Kim as she was entering his office and he also wave me into his office and said, "Praise the Lord," how are we doing." "Kim and I said, that we are bless and I also thanked him for preaching the word of the Lord. Everyone in that office was full of joy and peace but the Prophet joy and peace could be easily seen through his eyes. The conversation was so blessed and filled with the word of God. Doing the conversation, Kim said, to the man of god through the joy and peace that was taking place in that office. "Kim said everyone keep thinking that *"Love Forever"* and I are brother and sister." I was laughing about it in a joyful way and I also agreed with Kim that every one at church thought that Kim and I was sister and brother and sister. The Prophet said, "do you want me to tell you what the Spirit of the Lord has revealed to me." Kim and I said yes Sir. The Prophet said, "The Spirit of the Lord just revealed to me that you two are ordained to be together." The joy that Kim and I just received from the Prophet that came from God couldn't be stopped. I said to myself, "ordained to be together!" Kim and I." In a emotional way my mind was spending with happiness, joy and peace. Kim is a very beautiful woman and any man would be well please to be ordained to be with her. The only thing that I was sure of was getting my life on track and by learning how to live a godly life that is well pleasing to the Lord. The man of god just took my faith in God to a higher level that couldn't be stop, by heading toward the right path. The Lord had just sealed my faith with him by ordaining me to have a soon to be beautiful wife. I felt as though I was riding on a cloud of glory and the devil in hell couldn't stop the feeling I was having. We thanked the man of god greatly in a emotional way as we left the church being filled with the word of the Lord as well as the joy and peace we felt with the determination to live a godly life and to refuse to live a life of sin which is displeasing in the sight of the Lord. As days and weeks went by Kim and I, continued to go to church and to build our faith in the word of the Lord. The more we built our faith and learned how to live a godly life. The more our old friends begin to turn against us because we wasn't walking in a worldly manner, we was living godly to the best of each of our understanding. There was times that we was growing so close with the word of God and the relationship with the Lord that our family was starting to turn against us. I didn't have much understanding in those days that we was walking in the light of life is why that many was afraid or was a shame to be around us. (I later found out that people love darkness rather than light. JOHN 3 19 said, And this is the condemnation that light is come into the world, and men love darkness rather than light, because their deeds were evil.) So while Kim and I continued in the light, those that had not the light of life which is Jesus Christ living in them. The darkness became enemies against us. (people that's living a sinful life) Doing one Sunday while having a joyful time at church the Prophet would speak to Kim and I and ask her when will we be ready for marriage. We wasn't sure, because at that time Kim and I wasn't making good money. We was still trying to find the right job to make a living. We were both young and she lived with her mother and I lived with my mother. We was right across the street from each other.

The broken vows.

The Prophet told us to stop by his house so that we could receive the money from him for a marriage license. He would often preach about being married, and that it was better to marry then to sin in the sight of the Lord (CORINTHIANS 7 9 says, But if they can not contain, let them marry: for it is better to marry than to burn). As we arrived at the man of god house. We got out of the car and knocked on the door, someone from the church that was living with the Prophet came to the door and we ask him was the Prophet awake. The guy said, "Just one minute let me go and see." Two minutes later the guy came back and told us that we would have to wait for awhile. So we waited. Until this time Kim and I had never had sex together even before we started going to church together. There was a time when we came close but we never did because her mother came home right at that time. Although we would have sex with other people and party we never had sex together with each other when we was living our life as a sinner. The Prophet finally came to the door and greeted us and gave Kim the money for the marriage license. We gave our thanks and then headed to the court house to get the marriage license. We was so happy and excited, neither one of us had ever been married before. So not only was I going into this marriage with Kim, I was going into this marriage with her son Mike as well as she was going into this marriage with my two daughters. Mike was only a year old.

I had my mind made up that I was going to be a great husband and a great father to Mike and my two daughters. I was so happy, joyful and excited about trusting the Lord to make it all happened. I felt like I was flying in the sky and couldn't be stop because I had the Lord on my side. As we entered the court house. We filled out the paper work that was necessary to be filled out for the marriage license. We laugh and ask each other question of one another family information. We completed the forms and left the court house. (The wedding was scheduled for the following Wednesday night.) I went home to my mother house and read my bible as Tuesday began to turn into Tuesday night. I continued on reading my bible and then the phone ringed. I answered the phone to only hear Kim sweet voice on the other side, for some reason her voice sounded sexy as she spoke through the phone into my ear. "She said, "What are you doing?" I told her that I was sitting around studding the word." "She said, "in a sexy voice, we could study together if you want to come over." I said, "that I would be there in a minute." Kim said, okay" and then I got off the phone with her sexy voice still ringing in my head. I felt like I was traumatize as her voice ran through my body, mind and soul and settled in my spirit as though a spell had been placed on me, a spell of a sexual force.

I made it to Kim house in five minutes. I knocked on the door as Kim opened the door. I was amazed at how beautiful she was looking and how sexy she looked in that dress that she was wearing. My emotions and feelings was running wild. I was walking strong in the Lord to the best of my ability. It has been months since I had even thought about sex. She told me to come inside and as I walked into the house. I gave her a hug and my heart started beating very fast. My sex drive was very high. Just the touch from that hug took my breath away. She must have notice the heat between us because while we hugged. She looked into my eyes and smiled and gave me a look of understanding as though she also was saying that it has been along time since she had sex as well. After we hugged we pass the living room into another den like living room and we talked for a little and she ask me did I want some of her mother fruit salad. "I said sure," because her mother could make the best fruit salad that I had ever tasted in my life. As I ate the fruit salad and watch how beautiful Kim was as she walked back and forward into the kitchen from the den. I had forgotten all about studying the bible with her. We talked about our marriage and how excited we were to be getting ready to get married the next night. It was a night before that Kim and I would be married. I helped Kim put up the plates. As our bodies stood next to each other. I gave Kim a hug while we was standing in the kitchen and our heart beat's begin to beat a little more faster. Emotions once again started running wild, because of the heat that we was causing each other couldn't be put out by the coldest winter night. The heat became more and more intensified until our bodies became a sexual flame. I found myself placing Kim on top of the kitchen counter as our hands began to rub on each other bodies. As I slowly begin to lift up Kim's dress, to my surprise she wasn't wearing anything underneath her dress. My sex drive begin to swell until the fullness of it's desire. Neither one of us tried to stop the other. Kim welcome me to proceed. We had sex on top of the kitchen counter. While we was having sex, many thoughts came to my mind of trying to justify the wrong that we were doing. I also became nervous. I couldn't help but to think that Kim mother would come down stairs at any moment, but thank god she never did. We sexed each other until ecstasy. When we was finish. We looked into each other eyes and Kim said, ooooooooooooooooooooowwhhh, look what we did and I said to myself we knew that this was wrong but such justifying thoughts tried to cover up the guilty feelings. (that wasn't easy to do) I thought to myself and said, "what do it matter anyway we will be getting married tomorrow night anyway." I said, "goodnight to Kim and we both left each other with a kiss and a smile on our face but still with the guilt feelings for committing a sinful acted in the sight of the Lord. I went home and prayed for forgiveness. The next day Kim and I met up and we went to the store so that she could buy a dress that would match my suit that I would be wearing to our wedding. I had a light brown cream color suit that she wanted to be that the dress she bought would match with my light brown cream colored suit. When Kim Found the right dress that would match. We left the store and went home to prepare ourselves for our marriage that would be taking place later that evening around 7:30 pm. As I walked into my mother house she greeted me and asked me how did I feel about getting married. That whole day I had been having a strange feeling even when Kim and I was together buying that dress for our wedding. The closer time began to move toward that evening that we would be married. I felt something in my heart saying no! don't do it! don't get married, You are making a big mistake! What are you doing, can you not feel the stop sign that's place on your heart that's saying no! don't do it!. I told my mother that I didn't feel right. I said, " I have a funny feeling in my heart." I had never felt like this before. This feeling was much more stronger than any guilt feeling that I ever had and this wasn't a guilt feeling. This was a feeling that I couldn't explain because from my understanding. I was ordained to merry this woman. I was ordained by the Lord through a Prophet. I told my mother even though I felt this way I just wanted to do what was right in the sight of the Lord. So if the Lord order this marriage I said I must obey no matter what I was feeling. Time had come so that it was time for me and my soon to be wife to get married. Though I had that bad feeling. I was encouraged from the words, ordained to be together as the scripture speaks of the goodness of finding a wife. (PROVERBS 18 22 says Whoso findeth a wife findeth a good thing, and obtaineth favour of the Lord.). Surely I knew that I was bless and couldn't be stopped. Surely I was looking forward of receiving favour of the Lord. I was ready to make it happened. I call Kim and asked her was she ready and she said, "Hello *Love Forever,* I'm getting ready now, meet me outside in ten minutes." "I said, okay," and we hung up the phone. Ten minutes later I walked across the street to meet Kim. Many people in the neighborhood saw us and knew that we had been going to church and that we was seeking for a change and that we was getting married that day. Some of the people in the neighborhood that knew us was happy for us. Some of the people had looks of envy in their eyes and didn't care one way or the other. But what matter to me was to do the will of the Lord and to be bless. I didn't care what other people thought, neither did Kim. There was a time when Kim and I came back from church her mother and my mother was so much against us going to that church and learning from the Prophet that they begin to show hatefulness toward us. One night the argument got so bad that as I was going through it Kim would also be going through the same thing at the same time. We both met up with each other outside and sat in her car. Doing those troublesome times Kim would start up her car and just star driving with no thought of where we was going. She drove for 30 minutes and parked, we ended up on a bridge where people would come and park their car and fish. We talked for a few minutes and closed our eyes as we held hands until the sun came up.

As I met up with Kim across the street to her mother house from where my mother was staying. We got in the car and drove to the Prophet house where we would be married. When we got there, there was also another couple getting married that same evening. They was up first for their ceremony and of the sealing of becoming husband and wife. We watch them with a smile on our faces and excitement with love and peace. Then we was called up for our ceremony to begin and take place. Kim and I looked into each other eyes and a minister from the church performed the routine that was needed. I was surprise when I looked around at all the people and saw that my Dad was there, because we never had any kind of a relationship. He never supported me. We was like strangers from the time I was born until the time I became a man. Kim mother and grandmother was there and also her sister with much hate in her eyes toward me. I never understood why her sister never like me. I didn't know her and she didn't know anything about me. My mother never showed up. I believe that she was against the whole marries thing. The only thing that was on my mind and heart was to please the Lord and do what he had call me to do regardless of how I felt or the bad feeling that was pulling at my heart earlier that day. With all my heart, mind, body and soul. I just wanted to do what was right, that was my #1 aim. I just wanted to be the best husband and the best father that any woman could ever wish for.

As Kim and I looked into each other eyes and said those magical words that would sealed our oneness with each other. I do!. When the ceremony was done. We went about greeting everyone. I greeted Kim's family and the people of the church. I also greeted Kim's sister (Shay) Who rolled her eyes at me and never said a word. While we was greeting everyone the lady from the first couple that was being marriage approached Kim as I stood near, with excitement the lady greeted Kim and said, "Girl how you doing?." This lady was so excited. She spoke a few more words to Kim and said, "I will see you later girl if you know what I mean, I got to go home to my husband. Kim loved to say those words as well (husband) because it was new to her just as saying well as saying the words wife was new to me and it felt good to say. I had the favour of the Lord. I was married, it was a done deal. I had did what I was told from the man of god to do. It was such a blessing. I would be with this beautiful woman for the rest of my life, and I was happy and well please. We couldn't be stopped. Until death did us apart. This part of my life was like the sweeties poem that ran through my mind and heart. A poem of a blessing that just been sealed. Until Death, Until death do us apart, there will always be a place, deep in my heart. Where passion is in the mist, and love do exist I hope you remember this, until death we will kiss.

Until death do me end, you're be my soulmate and not my friend, well make sweet love, from beginning, until the end. You're be my heavens, free from sin. Places we will go. Loving you is the most. Until death takes this ghost. I'll never let you go. Please don't tell me no. Forever our love will grow. Until death I'll love you so, I hope you feel the same way. Until death stop's this show! Those were my feeling from a day that was so perfected, a day that the Lord had made. I ask Kim was she ready to leave. She said, "in a minute." I was so excited that I finally would be free from the sin of sex, no longer would I have to worry or feel guilty for having sex. I was eager to get my wife home to make love to her and celebrate our special day together. As my wife and I greeted everyone, we got into the car and headed home. Our new home that we would be living in together. We moved into a apartment together. As we was walking up the stairs, I couldn't help but to think about my kids mother and how she would react to the news of me being married. That thought was pushed out of my mind as my wife and I proceeded up the stairs to our apartment. We smiled as we entered our apartment and started putting things together such as the bed and the pictures, and other things. When we was finished. We laded in the bed together. It was a lovely and peaceful night. Kim whispered in my ear and I begin smiling and feeling the heat that was running through our bodies as my sex drive started dancing to the call of love. That night we made godly love for the first time in our life. We had no worries of committing any sin from such godly love making. We made love for hours and felled asleep together from being exhausted. I woke up the next morning feeling bless with a smile on my face. My eyes was still closed as I move my hand around the bed to feel for my wife. I felt nothing so I opened my eyes and didn't see my wife, the bed was empty. I thought to myself, maybe she's in the kitchen cooking breakfast for us?. I got out of the bed and walked into the living room calling for my wife. Kim! Kim! heeeaaaaaay Kim!. There was no sound to be heard. I checked the bathroom just to be sure, not only was there no sound to be heard, but there was no Kim. Surely she would have woke me up if she was going somewhere?. Surely she would have let me know something?. Maybe she went to buy breakfast? I waited, hours had passed, morning turned into evening. I thought to myself, something's isn't right. I started feeling that bad feeling creeping up on me, that same feeling that was in my heart the day of our wedding.

I decided to leave our apartment in search for my wife, to find out what was going on. I walk over to her aunts apartment that wasn't to far from our apartment. I knocked on the door and her aunt came to the door. I said, "Hello Mrs. Joy, how are you?." She said, I'm fine." I said, "Have you seen Kim?. I haven't seen her all day." I woke up this morning to find her nowhere to be found. "Mrs. Joy said, "I'm getting ready to go to church, maybe she will be there." Do you want to ride with me to church?. "I said, yes ma'am, I will go with you, maybe she will show up at church tonight."

Mrs. Joy and I got into her car and headed to church. As we pulled up to the church, a lot of people was already there. We could her singing as Mrs. Joy and I got out of her car and walked closer to the doors of the church and, we went inside and took a seat. As I looked around for my wife, she was nowhere to be found. I thought to myself, where could she be, Lord I hope that she is okay, wherever she may be. "I'll just wait for a while and get into the service." While the service was going, someone from the church tapped me on the shoulder and said, "the Prophet would like to see you in his office. I stood up and walk toward the Prophet office. I knocked on the door and he said, "come in and have a seat." I sat down and looked at the Prophet he looked at me and then he begin to speak." He said, "*Love Forever,* I have something to tell you." I don't know if you are going to be able to handle what I'm about to say?" I said, "to myself, Lord God what is it now? (not knowing where my wife was at the time was more than enough to take to handle right now)" The Prophet said, "It's about your wife." There wasn't anything happy or joyful about the tone of his voice.

"He said, "are you going to be able to handle what I'm about to tell you about your wife." I said to myself again, Lord have mercy. "I hope she isn't dead?" So many thoughts was going through my mind." He said, "it was just revealed to me that your wife ran off with this guy." I have his name. I found out that he also has outstanding warrants, what do you want to do." Now my head was spending. I said to myself, ran off with another guy! We just got married, this can't be happening, not to me. How,? What?. I didn't understand. We just said vows to each other, until death do us apart. How could this be? Surely the man of god said that we was ordained by God to be together? What happened? As the church service went on while the Prophet spoke to me." He said, "I believe I know where they are." Let's get in my truck and go over there We got into the Prophet truck and as he drove to the location. I couldn't believe what was happening to me Surely I didn't do anything wrong? Surely I was only doing what the Lord had ordain me to do. We arrived where the Prophet had took m, where he believe they may be. We was at my wife mother place. The Prophet and I got of his truck and proceeded to the door. He knocked on the door continually. Know one came to the door as he kept on knocking while I stood by and saw a curtain move but. nobody came to the door. We got back into the truck and went back to the church. Doing the ride back to the church, the Prophet encouraged on how strong I was on handling the news of the situation with my wife.

A vow had been broken. I didn't know what to think. My mind had so many thoughts running around in my brain I didn't know what to do. We made it back to the church and I sat there for a little while and than I left. I went to my mom's house until I could get myself together. A week had passed, and talk was going around the neighborhood that the guy that my wife was with had been shoot at by someone in the neighborhood. It was also said that the guy had been arrested by the police for the warrants that he had. I never met the guy nor have I ever seen him but the people in the neighborhood had. I left my mother house to met up with my kids mother. (Faye) We had stop seeing each other doing the time Kim and I started going to church together and got married. I was at work and I call Faye to pick me up from work so we could talk. When my work hours was done. I clocked out and met Faye outside of my job. I got into her car and sat there for a minute. (Faye had no knowledge of what was going on in my life since we had been apart from each other). "I slowly begin talking." I told her that I love her and that I was sorry that we had been apart. I was trying to make peace with Faye as much as I could before I told her what was eating at my heart. I couldn't stand the feeling that was on my heart as I talk to Faye. (A feeling of having betrayed someone I loved). I never was in love with my wife even when we got married. She never gave me a chance to grow into falling in love with her. My only means were to do what the Lord had call me to do, what I was ordained to do. I didn't like the betrayal feeling that I was having that was eating at my heart. I couldn't take it anymore. So I said. "Faye. I have something to tell you, but before you get mad at me." I want you to listen to me carefully, please just listen okay. "We looked each other in the eyes and my heart melted away as I seen the love in Faye eyes, the love she had for me." I said, I got married but I'm not with her anymore and the only reason I got married was because when I started going to this church, a Prophet that was there told me that I was ordain to be married to this woman and bam!! before I could go on any more of what I was saying. Faye had slap me across the face hard and said, "You just going to up! and jump! and get married because some man told you to, are you crazy. How could you do this to me! how could you do this to us! Love Forever! I'm pregnant, with your son! I felt so bad. I was so upset with myself and so confused and so disappointed in myself of the things I had allow to happened. I told Faye over and over and that I was sorry. I told her I wanted to make it right. She gave me a chance. We drove to my mother house to pick up my clothes and things. I wanted to try and work it out with someone that I was in love with. I moved in with Faye and as days and weeks pass by. We begin to work on our relationship. Things started getting better. I had gotten a better job and in no time. I became the supervisor on my job. I made more money but I neglected going to church. Our relationship became stronger and our love grew.

CHAPTER 2

THE DOWN FALL

While my relationship with Faye was growing stronger and I begin to make better money and more money. I started sliding back into my old ways and such. I started doing drugs and selling drugs as well, I started having get together drug parties with worldly friends. The burden of loosing my wife and trying to have a understanding of what went wrong, laid on my heart heavy. I couldn't blame God because he wasn't the one that ran off my wife, she was the one that ran off, and when she did I ran away from living for the Lord. I would take care of home and make sure the bills were paid and things. I would go party, It was a long time before Faye found out that I was partying and selling drugs here and there. I hid it from her for along time but she was starting to close in on me. She would find lil baggies of cocaine that would fall out of my packet or that I would misplace. One day as I was using her car to go pick up some drugs and money, as I returned back home from my pick up. A bag of cocaine fell out of my socks with out me knowing about it, and was loss in her car. I pulled up in the driveway and I went into our house. I spoke to Faye and she said, I will be right back. I'm going to the store. She left and came within 15 minutes and she entered our house. She walked right up to me and slap the bag of cocaine on my chest, She said, "you need to be careful with your stuff, don't leave nothing like that laying around, do you understand me. I said yeah baby I'm sorry about that. I begin to think of, how did I allow myself to slip up like that?. I got to be more careful. I didn't want to end our relationship because of my foolishness. (maybe she went light

14

on me because I was bringing in good money) Whatever the reason was, I needed to be more careful. I am already high and been drinking and the only reason I'm covering up my highness is because of the alcohol, but I got a feeling that she knows I'm doing something because when we have sex I can't get enough and my ever words are penetrating to her soul and that's because I'm deeply in love with her and when I get high my true feelings would come out and my sex drive would last for hours. That night we made love, I knew that she was tired because we was love making until the sun started coming up. I know we both had to go to work but as long as I was taking her to higher levels of love, the more she refuse to say no. We couldn't get enough of each other. As Faye stomach begin to grow larger. She took leave from work. I came home to her and she said, "will you be able to take care of all the bills. (since she was on leave) I said yeah because I was making good money at my job and plus I was selling drugs on the side. I began paying all the bills. One day I came home from work, having just been paid. I ask Faye what was the total of all the bills?. After she gave me the total. I laid the money out on the bed for the bills. She went through everything and said, "what about the phone bill?." I said, "I don't use your phone at all and you know that." I had my own cell phone from the job that I would use. So we got into a big argument over the phone bill that I didn't want to pay because I never used it. Faye being very emotional begin to cry and that made me feel like I didn't love her. She knew how to melt my heart with her tears. I just didn't like to see any woman cry. My heart melted away and I said, "here." I gave her the money for the phone and then I left and went to party. I felt like I was on top of the world but I knew deep down inside that I was living a sinful life and I didn't care. I had received to much disappointment in my life to care about how I was living.

August 10, 2004. My son was born. I was so happy, (it was me Faye Shataura Maya and M.J) We were one big happy family. I always promised my kids mother that I would never be a stranger to none of my kids like my dad was to me and my brothers. I loved my kids dearly. How could anyone be a stranger to their own flesh and blood. That one I will never know. I began to build a great relationship with my kids as months passed by, but I also began to get sloppy with my uses of drugs and making drug sells. Faye was starting to get fed up with me leaving the house in the middle of the night to make a sell and to have drug parties that she was unaware of, but had a strong feeling about. She knew that I would smoke weed from time to time and she was okay with it as long as I was bringing money home. She ones tried smoking weed with me one time but I didn't want her to do it because that day for the first time, I had put some cocaine mix with my weed. I was on the back porch and I was smoking weed mix with cocaine when Faye open the door to the back porch and said, "what's up, what you doing?," I said, "just smoking a little weed. Faye took me by surprise when she said, "let me try some. I thought to myself, here we go. I didn't know what to do, I didn't want to get caught. So I watch her with a guilty look on my face. My heart was saying please don't smoke it to hard if you are going to smoke it. She looked at me with the guilty look on my face and said. "Do you what! I said, "do you know what you're doing." She said, "I got this and she was smoking that weed like she was in a movie. She passed me the blunt back to me and went back inside. That night we made sweet love while listening to some *Love Forever* gaye coming from the radio (the song distance lovers). I never would have thought in a million years that one day our love would be distance. Had I knew, I would have change a lot of things about the way that I was living. One pay day weekend, I paid the bills and left the house. I was partying so hard that I didn't come back home until the sun started coming up. I had got a friend to lie for me by telling Faye that I would be out of town working. Faye brothers the lie but that morning when I returned home. I was so high I looked like Michael Jackson video thriller. My lips was chapped and I had drunk so much alcohol that you could look me in the face and see that I was intoxicated. Surely she knew that I had lied and have not been out of town working. She gave me a look that could kill. As the day went by she would not speak to me and when I spoke to try and see could I get a response from her, it only made things worse. She told me to leave so I left. I stayed gone for a week and I told her that I was sorry and we made sweet love. Two months went by and our relationship was going okay so I felt okay. I was still working and selling drugs, sometimes I would sell to my neighbor. One morning while Faye was taking me to work we had a much heated argument. I got out the car and went to work. When I got off work and went to the job site, there was a cop car park in the parking lot of the job site. I said to myself I wonder why the police is seating out there. To my surprise when I came of the door to the warehouse from the job site. The police got out of his car and walked up to me and said, "are you Love Forever?. I said," yes Sir, the officer had papers in his hands. He handed me the papers and said, "A retraining order had been file against you by a Miss Faye. I couldn't believe it. I thought to myself, why would she do that. It was just a argument and not a fight. I wasn't the kind of man that would hit a woman. My mother had raised me better than that. I couldn't believe that she would do that. We even kissed when I got out of the car this morning, (dang!) Why would she do something like that. I didn't hurt her by pity my hands on her or anything. Their was only one time that I could remember ever slapping Faye, and that was when we got into a argument that I thought that it wasn't a heated argument at all. Out of nowhere doing the argument, Faye had sprayed me with mace and all at the same time while I had been sprayed. My hand grabbed her while my eyes were close. I wasn't even that upset until I heard my baby boy coughing in his room from the spray that Faye had sprayed. While my eyes were close and hearing my son cough. I slap Faye and said," how could you be so stupid? Why would you spray me? are you crazy? you got my son coughing from this stuff. She said", I'm sorry," I said, "I know you are, how could you. (At that time I just needed to get away) I was so upset with myself for slapping her. I felt guilty, so I took her car keys and said, "we need to cool off for a minute." So I left for two hours. I just went and drove and for some reason, I ended up parking the car at the church.

The same church my ex wife and I would attain. I went into the church and entered the bathroom. I could hear the Prophet preaching. I was so ashamed to leave the bathroom and join the church service. So I stay and listen inside the bathroom. While I was listening, someone had entered the bathroom. When I looked up. I realize that it was my oldest brother (Plook) standing there He had became a minister at the church. He said, "brother, how you doing." I said, "not good, I just came to listen." He said, "I haven't seen you in a while. (he never looked down on me/for returning to the church) He said, "want you come on into the service, the Prophet and everyone would be happy to see you." So I said, "okay, give me a minute. He left the bathroom and I knew that the Lord had put it on his heart for me to attain the service. I left the bathroom and listen to the Prophet on forgiveness of sin, and when he was done he ask, did anyone needed prayer. I went up for prayer. He place oil on my head and prayed for me as while my eyes were close and my heart was fixed on being forgiving from the Lord. When he finished praying for me, he said that it was good to see me and he wanted to remind me that the Lord loves me ant that the Lord is married to the back slider, he stated that from the word of God in the book of JEREMIAH 3 14 It says, Turn, o backsliding children, saith the Lord for I am married until you. I left the church and drove back to the house. I was feeling good. When I pulled-in the drive way. I still had oil on my head and it was shining. I said to myself, that I was going to leave the oil there so when Faye see it she want have any kind of thoughts that I was left the house to go sell drugs or party. As I got out the car and went in the house it was a peaceful night. Faye was laying on the bed. So I got into the bed right beside her. She looked at me crazy. So I smile and she said, "where you been?," I said, "I been to church, you don't believe me?." look!. I let her see the church oil that was on my head. I held her and we went to sleep. That was the only time that I remember slapping Faye. As I stood there with the retraining order in my hand that I couldn't believe that I was holding. The officer said, "Have a nice day. I call my cousin to pick me up so that I could go get my things from Faye place. They arrived and I got my things and checked into a hotel for a few days. As weeks passed, Faye and I got back together but my party life was closing in on me. I know that I wasn't living right and yet that small voice that was in my heart was warning me to get myself together. My secret party life had put the flame out from that small voice that was in my heart. Faye and I would argue, break up, and get right back together. Our life together was like a marry- go- round. (I never thought that one day. it would come to a end).

The Chastening.

One day after work, I came home and I started getting high. I would sneak around Faye to get high. I would tell her that I'm going to the store and I would bring back a beer. I some times would go into the bathroom when she would be on the phone talking. Those were my chances to get out of her eye sight and get high. Sometimes I would take chances. I would go sit on the porch to smoke some weed or take a smoke break. I would snort some cocaine as fast as I could because I knew that it was a chance that she would come to the door to see what I was doing. That night we made love together into the morning of the raising of the sun. I was off that day but she had to work. Through that night night I was so high that I could hear my heart beat through my ears and I was afraid that she would hear it also. I was paranoid. My heart was beating hard and I couldn't sleep. So I had to lay there and play like I was asleep. With my eyes close until the next day, until she left for work. As the morning came, she got ready for work and I just laid there as though I was asleep. But I couldn't wait until she would leave because my partying was just getting started. She left the house and I got out of to look out the window to be sure that she was gone. As soon as I knew that I was in the clear. I pulled out a plate and started chopping up some cocaine. When I was done I took a nice big snort of some of the cocaine, and as soon as I was in the motion of taking that snort. I never heard Faye car come back to the house nor did I hear her open the door and walk into the house. As I sat there in the living room and saw the sun light shine in the living room from the door. I look up and see Faye looking right at me. (I thought to myself, man, she finally caught me and their is know lie that I could make up for this one). She look at me I look at her with a tear that slides down my face from being high from the cocaine. I was busted. There I sat with a plate filled with cocaine as Faye and I looked at each other. I knew that their was a chance that she would find out but never like this. Never did I think that she would catch me in the very act. My heart fell to my stomach as Faye watch me watch her. I will never forget that look on her face. A look of rejected love, a look of betrayal. (I thought to myself, how could I have let this happened. How did I get caught up into this secret party life) Most of my friends that snorted cocaine, their wife's and girlfriends knew that they did it, and it was okay as long as they was taking care of home. But Faye wasn't that kind of woman. She was a angel, how stupid could I be. I knew that I had hurt the one that I loved and the one that loved me. I had disappointed her and that wasn't cool at all. As we looked at each other Faye looked at me and shook her head from side to side and walked into the bedroom to get something and then left and walked back out the door. I quickly put up the plate with the cocaine and ran to the door to outside to her car were she was sitting. I said, "Faye I'm so sorry." I didn't know what else to say because I was busted. I had failed at being a family man. I had failed at being a father/lover. She said, "When I get back home we need to talk. I knew that it wasn't going to be a good talk because I had failed and in so many ways. I had betrayed the one that I love with my secret party life. I knew that it was getting out of hand because I remember a time that I was so close to getting caught that it was only by the mercy of God that I didn't get caught. It was one evening that Faye had dropped me off at my mother house. Instead of her driving all the way to my mother house. I had her to drop me off close by and I told her that I would walk the rest of the way. I enter this party house were parties take place all the time. After Faye was out of sight I went there and stayed there until night fall. While I was there a woman and I that own the house t together and started drinking. One thing lead into another and we both ended up in the bed together in her room with the door closed. While we was having sex, the party continued to go on in the living room. For some strange reason. I could hear my kids mother Faye calling my name and then there was a knock on the door as my name continued to go out from her mouth. I said to the woman I was with I said, "don't open the door." I quickly put on my clothes and my name and the knocks at the door continued to get louder. The woman that I was with was known for putting woman in their place and I didn't want this woman to hurt Faye, because I never seen this woman loose a fight to no female.

The woman that I was with said, "you better do something before I do. (I said to my self think?) I went over toward the bed room window and tried to lift the window up but the window was stuck. The window had been hammered down to keep the window from being push open. I thought that for sure that I was going to get caught. I didn't want to get caught like that, for sure Faye heart would be broken. (but the mercy of God) With all my might I push as hard as I could and the hammered down window came open, the window opened up. I jump out the window and ran toward my mother house. The whole time that I was running, Faye was still inside the party house. She never saw me. She never saw me enter the house nor leave so I was in the clear. I could say what I wanted to say, so I thought. When I made it down the street to my mother house. I open the door and went in. My mother said, "Faye had just left looking for you." I said, "when she come back tell her that I was in the back room sleeping and you didn't know. My mother got mad and said, "I'm not going to be in the middle of your mess, you need to straighten your self up!. Faye returned back to my mother house and I came outside and told her that I was in the back room sleep. But she didn't believe it. (She had no proof). When Faye came home from work she told me to leave. I left and we went through the marry- go- round- again. We ended up right back together after a week went by but the chastening of the Lord was at hand. One night I needed to go pick up some money. I was high but not super high. I ask Faye could I use her car to go pick up some money. She said, "no and we got into a big argument about it. I said, "you mean to tell me that I'm paying bills on a car I can't use." Faye said, "no, it's late, I don't want you to go, you are not using my car. So I sweet talk my way into using her car to go pick up some money. I got in the car and I was on my way, so I thought. As I was driving, it begin to rain just a little. I look up ahead of the road and notice a cop car in front of me. I kept on driving as well as the cop car. While the cop car was driving in front of me. I notice another cop car to the right up ahead, this cop car was park sideways facing the road. But what I didn't know was that the cop car in front of me would park sideways as well facing the other cop car (like two birds that are facing each other, to give the other bird the worm, face to face) As I continue to drive as the cop car drove in front of me. All of a sudden the cop car hit his breaks without putting on his turning signal and made a hard right to face bumper to bumper with the other cop car that was parked off the road, but on the right side of the road. When I notice the cop car that was in front of me, hit breaks. I also hit breaks but because of the light rain that night the car began to slide. There was nothing else for me to do at that moment but to hope that some how the car would stop sliding, it never did, I continued to slide just as the cop car was pulling in, to face the other cop car, bumper to bumper. Just as the cop car was face, waiting to meet the other cop car so that they could park bumper to bumper, and they parked that way. Ten seconds later as Faye car continued to slide. I made a right to avoid the on coming cars that was on my left. So as I made a right while the car continued to slide. I crashed right between the cop cars, both of the bumper to bumper cop cars opened up like the white ball on a pool table that opens up and knock loose all the other balls that's stuck together. The cars opened up both cop cars and I went straight between the two cars as the cars was being opened by Faye car. I couldn't believe what had just happened. I knew that my world had just ended. There will be no more marry-go-rounds with Faye. I had crashed her car and I knew that she would hate me for the rest of her life. (what have I done) I didn't have any license. So I knew that I was going to jail. (how stupid was I) I said to myself, not without a fight.

As the car made it through the middle of the two cop cars. Faye car was spending out of control. I straightened the stirring wheel and gain control of the car. Then I hit the gas and tried to drive away from the seem. As I went speeding down the street doing 60 MPH and above. I looked into the mirror and saw other cop cars coming fast. I thought to myself, the cop cars that I crashed into must have call it in (dang!).

As the other cop cars got closer. They was using the front bumper of their cars to try and hit the side of my back bumper. Every time they would try and hit my back bumper. I would see it and sway the car from being hit by the cop cars as I speed up along the road. I ran through red lights to try and get away but then the back tire blow out and the car engine went out. I turn the car to the left and the car continues to coast down a back road doing 50 mph as the cop cars gained up on me. I stop the car while making a hard right turn into someone's yard as the car came to a complete stop. I look behind me through the car window as the cop cars approach me from the driver side door by blocking me in on the driver side with his car bumper. I reach for the passenger door. I opened it and took off running while leaving the car behind me. As I ran I saw tall bushes up ahead. There was no where else for me to go. The cops was gaining up on me. I ran straight into the bushes while jumping in the air. If I had known what was behind the bushes. I would have came up with a better plan. As I jump through the bushes while flying in the air. I could hear the officers shoot their stun guns at me as they went pass my ear as they tried to stop me from running. In the air flying through bushes, I was suddenly hit in the stomach as I was flying in the air through the bushes. - on the other side of the bushes was stacks of wood that been chopped and stacked metal on the other side of the bushes which cause me to hit a front ward flip as I went through the air and through the bushes and hit the wood that was stacked behind the bushes. I hit the ground hard, out of breath. I said to myself, I give up, I can't run no more. The officer cuffed me and took me to the Escambia county jail. That night I made the news. I was on T.V. My sins had been exposed, so that the whole world could see. I wasn't proud of that at all. I had let down so many people. Even though I had stop going to church, many people at the church had faith that I would do better, but I was only doing worse I knew that they was praying for me, but I had became addicted to a sinful life style. The Judge sentence me to a work release program that was across the street from the county jail. I sign myself out of the county jail and I walked across the street to the work release program just as the Judge had ordered me. I got there and entered the place and sign myself in. The work release program is a place where you have one foot in jail and one foot in freedom. The only time you had a little freedom is when you was allowed to go to work. I was sentence there for three months by the Judge. Had I known what was ahead of my life to come. I would have complete the program and got my life on the right path.

CHAPTER 3

ISAIAH 30 1

Woe to the rebellious children, saith the Lord, that take counsel, but not of me and that coved with a covering, but not of my spirit, they may add sis to sin.

The Lord was very merciful to me but even sometime I could find myself misusing the mercy of the Lord by choosing sin rather than a life with the Lord. A life of holiness and rightful living. So here I was at this work release program. I would leave the work release program every morning but I was off on the weekends and I would be stuck in that place with nothing to do. I was so much addicted to living a sinful life style, that I would sometimes find a way to party again while being at this work release program. As I started going to work and returning to the work release program place. I would tell my program worker that I had to see. I would tell her that my work hours were later than they really were I did that so that I could have time to party. As long as I came back to the place when I got off work than, everything was cool. While being there, everyone that is sentence there have to sign papers and one of the papers we were to sign was a form stating that if we leave that place and do not come back in the right time frame that's due, than they would charge whosoever that didn't follow there rules with escape, which could carry anywhere from seven to fifteen years. I was living in such a fast life that I sign the papers without ever taking time to read them. The only thing that was on my mind was to go party and partying is what I did. As I got off work one evening, I went into this apartment complex that's call

Truman apartments where I know a lot of people who loved for me to come and hang out with them, mostly woman because Truman apartments is a apartment complex for single mothers that's trying to better their self. Some of the woman loved me so much that a lot of them would give me a second key to their apartment just for me to come around. A lot of these women would do anything for me. They was crazy about me. A lot of them loved the sex that I would give them and others love the drugs that I could get a hold to, either way they was crazy about me. I was well known in that apartment complex. As I entered the gate where most people check in at before entering. I kept walking through the gate because at that time there wasn't any police cars at at the gate at this hour of the day. I had a guy from work let me off near the apartments. I went to my cousin apartment. I went in because the door was open and I greeted her. I said, "what's up Bridgett." She said, "what's up T.J. I went by the name of T.J when I entered these parts of Pensacola. I didn't think that it was important that women should know my real name, and besides all we ever did was party, get high and have sex. My cousin would put me down with some of her friends." I said to Bridgette, what's good with you? She said, "nothing much, I'm getting ready to go to bingo and try to win some money. I said, "win some for me when you go, hey what's up wit your friend Kiesha. She said, "boy that girl is like a cousin to me. I said, "well she's not my cousin. Bridgette said, "go talk to her. I said, "cool, that's what's up, I'll talk to her when I run across her, she always playing hard to get." Kiesha also live in the apartments complex. I said, "have you talk to Teiarra or Sky today?. Teiarra and Sky were sister and brother but good friends of Bridgette and I. "I talk to them earlier Bridgette said." I said, "okay I'm getting ready to go around there, I'll get up with you later cousin." I met up with Sky and Teiarra, they were happy to see me. Everybody was happy to see me. That would be normal routine. I would get off work and go hangout with friends every day and each time I would meet more people, more woman and party, party, party, and I would go back to the work release program on time and start everything all over the next day after work. At times I would bring a little cocaine into the work release program for the guys that would get high, just to pass some time. (had I known that my time would soon be up, I would had change a lot of things).

One day after getting off of work, I met up with Sky at the apartment complex (Truman apartments). I said, "what's up Sky." He said, "what's good. I said, "nothing much, and than I said, "hey you want to go to Kelly street and see what's popping, see can we make some money. Sky said, "yeah let's do that Sky said. Kelly was a street across from Truman apartments. When you left Truman apartments you would cross the street, a busy road that was in front of Truman apartments. As soon as you left the gate that was in front were you go in and out of the apartments complex. We left the apartments and cross the street and went on toward Kelly Street were everybody who wanted to buy or sell drugs could, but you couldn't hangout there long because the police were sure to ride the streets of Kelly to make a arrest upon anyone that didn't follow the law. Fifteen minutes later we were heading back to the apartment complex, as we were walking down the street a convertible pulled up with the top down with two beautiful white women inside. One was doing the driving and the other one was on the passenger side of the car. As we walked they slowed the car down and pull right up next to us. As I turn to look at the two beautiful white ladies. I thought to myself (dang!) they must be the police. (man!) I'm about to go to jail for sure. I know they saw us selling drugs. But to my surprise as I looked into the back seat I said to myself this can't be the police because why would they be driving around with a case of beer in the back seat. The one on the driver side spoke first, she said, "hey where are y'all headed. I said, across the street where those apartments are at, she said, "do you want a ride over there?. (it was a beautiful sunny day) I wasn't sure at first, but I change my mind I notice how the one on the driver side was looking me up and down as though I was her meal for today. I said, "that will be cool, what's your name? She said, "Christian and this my friend Sue, but you can call me Miss C, y'all jump in, I don't mine taking you two across the street. As Sky and I jump into the convertible. I began having a conversation with Miss C, who was driving, and Sky began having a conversation with Sue. I exchange cell phones # with Miss C as we entered the gates of Truman apartments. Many people that I knew was calling out my name as we rode pass them as though I was a celebrity. Miss C drop us off and left with a look on her face telling me to call as soon as I can. I left Sky and went walking through the apartment complex while pulling out my cell phone. I give Miss C a call. She pick up on the second ring and I said, "what's up, what are you doing, this is T.J She said with so much joy in her voice. O hello T.J I'm at home, do you want to hang out with me. I said, "yeah come through. Ten minutes later, Miss C pulled up and we left, we ended up at a clothes store and she told me to get anything that I wanted. The day was still beautiful, the sun was still out.

After we left the clothes store, to my surprise Miss C took me to a expensive restaurant. I thought to myself, man this woman is going all out for me. We sat and ate and left twenty five minutes later. We were at her house and the day begin to turn into night. Miss C took a shower and got into the bed. I got in the bed with her and told myself of all the things she did for me, at least I could give her what she wanted. That night I gave Miss C the best sex she ever had. We went to sleep together and the next morning she woke me up and gave me a second house key to her place. She told me that she would see me later. When she left, I also left and went back to Truman apartments with no thoughts of ever going back to the work release program. I had left that place two months ago.

One day I return from work and I was so high that I didn't want to be trapped in the work release place so to continue my party. I told the staff that worked there that I needed to go to the hospital, that was the only plan that I could come up with so that I could leave. That was the only way that they would allow me to leave because wants you are in from work your day is over with. You are locked into that place. I was so high that I didn't want my highness to go down. So I told the staff that I needed to go to the hospital and they said, "what's the reason." I told them that I was bleeding when I did a #2, which I really had started bleeding from eating so much hot and spicy food all my life. I had this issue before and was treated for it. I was suffering from internal hemorrhoids, at that time it would come and go but would cause me pain and the lost of blood. I called a cab and they pick me up ten minutes later. My plan was to go to the hospital and try and leave as soon as I could. When I got there I waited for my name to be call and as soon as it was call. I went to the back to see the doctor. They held me there for a long time. They said that my heart was beating to fast and I knew the reason why because every time the nurse would leave me alone from checking up on me. I would snort some cocaine. I decided to sneak out of the hospital and go to this other apartment complex that wasn't far from the work release place. Those apartment complexes were call Pensacola village. You could go there and make lots of money, it was a apartment complex where most people never sleep. I called a cab wit my cell phone and left the hospital. The cab dropped me off at the Pensacola village apartments. As I was walking through I made a few sells and ran across a lady name CC, she loved to party when she saw me. I said, "what's good CC she said, "heeeeeeeeeey T.J. where you been?." I said here and there, CC let's go to your place and party. She said, "say no more." when we got high and went to the Conner store that stayed open all night- After we left the clothes store, to my surprise Miss C took me to a expensive restaurant. I thought to myself, man this woman is going all out for me. We sat and ate and left twenty five minutes later. We were at her house and the day begin to turn into night. Miss C took a shower and got into the bed. I got in the bed with her and told myself of all the things she did for me, at least I could give her what she wanted. That night I gave Miss C the best sex she ever had. We went to sleep together and the next morning she woke me up and gave me a second house key to her place. She told me that she would see me later. When she left, I also left and went back to Truman apartments with no thoughts of ever going back to the work release program. I had left that place two months ago.

One day I return from work and I was so high that I didn't want to be trapped in the work release place so to continue my party. I told the staff that worked there that I needed to go to the hospital, that was the only plan that I could come up with so that I could leave. That was the only way that they would allow me to leave because wants you are in from work your day is over with. You are locked into that place. I was so high that I didn't want my highness to go down. So I told the staff that I needed to go to the hospital and they said, "what's the reason." I told them that I was bleeding when I did a #2, which I really had started bleeding from eating so much hot and spicy food all my life. I had this issue before and was treated for it. I was suffering from internal hemorrhoids, at that time it would come and go but would cause me pain and the lost of blood. I called a cab and they pick me up ten minutes later. My plan was to go to the hospital and try and leave as soon as I could. When I got there I waited for my name to be call and as soon as it was call. I went to the back to see the doctor. They held me there for a long time. They said that my heart was beating to fast and I knew the reason why because every time the nurse would leave me alone from checking up on me. I would snort some cocaine. I decided to sneak out of the hospital and go to this other apartment complex that wasn't far from the work release place. Those apartment complexes were call Pensacola village. You could go there and make lots of money, it was a apartment complex where most people never sleep. I called a cab wit my cell phone and left the hospital. The cab dropped me off at the Pensacola village apartments. As I was walking through I made a few sells and ran across a lady name CC, she loved to party when she saw me. I said, "what's good CC she said, "heeeeeeeeeey T.J. where you been?." I said here and there, CC let's go to your place and party. She said, "say no more." when we got high and went to the Conner store that stayed open all night - to go buy. We went back to her place and got drunk and super high. We had sex and passed out until the next day. I knew I had messed up. I should have went back to the work release place but I didn't and I knew that they was waiting on my return. I knew a warrant would soon be put out for my arrest, for not returning like I should have. I was feeling myself. I was enjoying the money, making, having a everyday party life style. I had got use to it, so I said, "the hell with that work release place. Two months later here I was hanging out with Miss C. I would go from Miss C house to Truman apartments and back and forward to and from Pensacola village making money and sexing the ladies. I had been on the run for a year and word would get around to me from people that I knew, that my mother would tell them to tell me to turn myself in. I just couldn't do it just because she wanted me to. I soon faded away from Miss C because I started meeting other women that wanted to do more for me than Miss C ever could. These women would make sure I kept money. They would always go out there way to do so.

CHAPTER 4

ROMANS 7 21-24

I find then a law that when I would do good, evil is present with me. For I delight in the law of God after the inward man: But I see another law in my members, warring against the law of my mind, and bringing me into captivity to the law of sin which is in my members. O wretched man that I am! who shall deliver me from the body of this death? I knew that I was living a fast life and I decided to slow down even though I had a warrant. I refused to turn myself in. One Sunday I decided to pay the church a visit. The church where I took the woman I married. I went there and felt some of the weight of the world come off of me. As I sat and listen to the word of faith that was being preach by the Prophet. When the service was coming to a closing. I went up for prayer. The Prophet place oil on my head and prayed for me. When he had finish. I left the church and decided to go visit with my cousin Bridgette. As I enter the gates of the Truman apartment complex and begin to walk to my cousin apartment. I notice a female approaching and I got closer. As she came into view. I notice that it was Keisha walking toward me with money on her shirt as she came near toward me. She said, "hello pastor." (I guess to her I looked like a pastor with my suit on)

I said, "what's up Keisha." She said, "it's my birth day." As she was saying this, she made sure that I would get a good look at the money that was pinned to her shirt but closer to her breast where her cleavage could be well seen. She said, "it's my birth day, are you going to give me some money for my birth day?." (Now Keisha was my cousin best friend they were more like cousin, the same Keisha that I tried to get to be one of my sex friends but she never gave me the time of day). I said, "yeah, so I reach in my suit pocket and pulled out a few dollars and gave it to her and she smile. I was surprise when she said, "can you come over to my apartment later and read the bible with me? I said, "sure, I'll be over there its no problem." I thought to myself, maybe she was save, that could be the reason why she never allowed me to be her sex friend. When I got to my cousin Bridgette apartment. I greeted her. We talk for a hour or so and then I left to head over to Keisha apartment. When I got there, I knock on the door She said, "come in, so I opened the door and entered her apartment. I sat down in the living room and she said, "I will be out in a minute. Two minutes passed by and Keisha came into the living room from her back bed room only wearing a robe with nothing underneath her robe. When I notice this I got up from the living room and started heading back to the door that I just entered. I said. "Keisha you know that I'm in the word, I'm not trying to go back into living my old life." I grab for the door nob. As I was doing so, Keisha block me off with her body. She than opened her robe and allowed her breast to be clearly seen. She place her breast right in my face as I begin to move away from her. Keisha said, "muuuuuum, muuuuuuumm, you are going to give me this right now. With the Sunday morning service oil still fresh on my head. I couldn't believe what was going on with her. Before I started going to church she wouldn't give me the time or day, now that I been going to church she threw her self at me. I said, "to myself, this is crazy. I need to get out of here. Keisha refuse to let me leave and on top of that the devil was playing tricks with my mind by telling me things such as you know you haven't had sex in a while, this is the woman that you been wanting for a while, go, go ahead and give it to her, give her what she wants, before she turns evil and do something wicked against you, with my mind spending from the pressure of the devil and the pressure of Keisha's throwing her self at me, with the Sunday service oil still fresh on my head. I failed weak to the pressure of it all and I gave into Keisha. She led me to her bed room where I got undress. She pull me on top of her and we begin having sex. (had I known the feeling that I would be feeling ahead of time I would have put up a better fight against this temptation). As we were having sex, I felt like I was trapped once again, trapped to the addiction of sin. (But I see another law in my members, warring against

31

the law of my mind, and bringing me in captivity to the law of sin which is in my members). The moment we finished having sex I felt a conviction like never before. I felt like the Lord had departed from me. I went back to my cousin Bridgette apartment and spent a night there. While I was there I tried to pray and it felt like the ears of the Lord was close to my prayers. I had never felt this way in my life. I felt so alone and empty inside. I felt so lost no matter how many times I prayed and begged for forgiveness. I just couldn't reach the Lord. I couldn't feel his spirit the way I felt it that Sunday morning. I closed my eyes and went to sleep in a state of sadness and disappointment for not doing what was right. (O wretched man that I am ! who shall deliver me from the body of this death).

The following night came around, the night of the week when church service were to be held on a Wednesday. I went and listen to the Prophet preach. The word of the Lord that he was preaching was just for me. He was preaching out the bible in the book of MATTHEW 5 13 it says Ye are the salt of the earth: but if the salt have lost his savour, where with shall it be salted? it is thenceforth good for nothing, but to be cast out, and to be trodden under foot of men. I knew that word came from God and it touch my heart in a convicting way. As weeks turn into a month. I slow down my fast living but that didn't last long because I had faded away from church again. I was young and stupid and had no wisdom at all but I knew that the Lord hands was still on me even when I didn't think that his hands were on me. I started back dealing with woman and selling drugs again.

CHAPTER 5

HEBREWS 12 6

For whom the Lord loveth he chasteneth, and scourgeth every son whom he receiveth. I continue to hang out at Truman apartments but I didn't know that I was getting ready to be punished by the Lord for running and living a life style of sin (because God hates sin). I met up with a old friend that I haven't seen in a long time, a partner of mine. His name was Fed, dark brown and wore his hair in dreadlocks Fed was known for getting into all kinds of trouble. It was a chance to take if you hung out with Fed because he made enemies. Fed loved to rob for his money and than he would party. As I was hanging out in the Truman apartments, Fed pulled up and said, "what's up," I said, "what's up Fed?, what you getting into?," He said, "nothing much just riding and smoking this good weed, what's up with you, you trying to roll?." I said yeah." I got in the truck that Fed was driving and we rode and smoke. Fed didn't really snort cocaine like I did but he would put it in his blunts mix with his weed. We stop and got something to eat and we smoked and drink a few beers that we got earlier at the corner store. Day turned into night and I passed out from being so high.

No matter where we went Fed kept a gun with him at all times because the life style that he was living, he never knew when his enemies would run down on him. As I was shaken awakened by Fed. He said, "look behind you, that look like the police. My heart started beating fast because I still had that warrant hanging over my head that I never took care of. Fed slowed the truck down and the car that was behind us slowed down as

33

well. We came to a stop and the car came to a stop as well. The car that was behind us flesh his car lights, then a man lend his head out the car and said, "police." Suddenly Fed punch on the gas to the truck and went speeding away. I said to myself (dang!) I shouldn't have never went riding with Fed. what the hell he got his self into. I got this warrant and I'm not trying to go to jail tonight. We went speeding away and turned here and there. We were losing the police car but only for a few minutes because other cop cars were call into the chase. Fed turned a another corner and told me to take his gun and throw it out the wind. I took the gun but I couldn't throw it out the window because the cop cars were right behind us. Soon Fed slowed the truck down just enough for me to jump out and run. I jump out with the gun in my hand and ran. As I was running I let the gun drop into the tall grass that I ran through. I ran into some bushes and ended up by a cliff down below the cliff was a lot of deep water. So I stayed hanging along the side of the cliff. I got down low so that the cops couldn't see me. The cops had stop their cop cars and got out to look for me on foot with their dog running beside them. They went through all the bushes and then suddenly they came to the cliff where I was hiding with my head low. The dog looked from right to left and then the officer shine his flashlight in my face. I came into the light of the flashlight and suddenly the officer notice me and then grab me by the back of the shirt and pull me up back on land from the cliff. When I was pull back to land, the officer began beating me with his flashlight as the dog began biting me on the butt. I yelled out through pain and the beating that I received. I thought for sure that I was a dead man. Blood began to pour out of my flesh from the powerful bites from the dog. I tried to stop the bites of the dog by grabbing his mouth but that didn't work because the dog bit my hand as well. The biting and the beating soon came to a stop. The officer picked me up and put hand cuffs on me I was then taken to the station where two detectives approach me. They ask me did I know anything about a shooting that took place. I didn't so they played bad cop/good cop with me, it's a game that the detectives tike to play to seek for the truth of the matter. One will act like a friend to help, and the other one would act like a enemy. I left the station and I was place into another police car where they also place Fed with me. The officer who arrested Fed had also beat him pretty bad.

His face and head was swelling greatly. They to us to the county jail. The next day I was seen by a Judge who then told me my charges and how much my bond was. My bond was to high to even think about, suddenly I felt like my life had come to a end. I didn't know what was going to happened. I had a bad feeling. I didn't know how to think. I felt like my life was over with. As I was taken back to my cell I begin praying. Many people at the county jail was face with a situation. I started reading my bible and began asking the Lord for forgiveness and to help me with this situation. Every morning I would get up early and read my bible and pray. Doing this time I had nobody on my side. My mother and I wasn't on best relationship terms because of how I was living when I was running in a wild life, a sinful life style. I wasn't receiving and money from anybody that knew me I couldn't buy canteen because of that reason. Only when I picked my bible up and got real with the Lord, then I started seeing changes. Many people in jail started seeing the change in me, even the staff's and the people that was in jail with me. Some of the people would come to my cell and we would read and study the bible together. It started off with one person coming to my cell and reading with me and praying with me and crying out to the Lord fro forgiveness. We would get together three times a week to study and pray. Most of the time I would minister the word of the Lord.

CHAPTER 6

PHILIPPIANS 4 19

But my God shall supply all your need according to his riches in glory by Christ Jesus. One day doing mail call I had received a letter from my sister Nora. She also had sent me some money so that I could buy canteen. I gave thanks to the Lord and wrote my sister back and told her how greatful I was of her writing me and sending me money for canteen. I knew in my heart that it was the power of God working through my sister to help me. The next couple of weeks that went by I got a letter from a long lost girl friend of mine who name was Rachael. She was very sweet, she also sent me money for canteen. She also came and visited with me a couple of times. She told me that she was reading the newspaper and came across my name and she said that she couldn't believes that I was in jail. Rachael stayed by my side for a while. A month or two later I get a letter from my mother and I write her back and told her that I was sorry and that I had messed up by allow myself to come to jail. My mother made sure that I would have canteen. Our relationship became stronger and I thanked the Lord for that. A week later my appointed by the courts lawyer came to see me.

She said, "how are you *Mr. Love Forever*. I shuck my head in a greeting way. Her name was Miss Patty. Miss Patty said, "that I had been charged with battery on a LEO, Robbery, aggravated battery with great bodily harm and escape. She also said that I was charged with car jacking and kidnapping. Miss Patty ask me what did I want to do because the state was offering me, If I pleaded guilty, 30 years. I said to myself, 30 years. I can't do 30 years. My whole life would be over, all my love one's that I surely would miss, O God help me, this can't be happening to me. What am I going to do. Miss Patty said, "I could take the case to trial. I told Miss Patty that we will go to trial. She said, "that the kidnapping and car jacking would be a different case. So I will be having two trials. I said, "Okay." Miss Patty left and I went back to my cell and prayed like never before. Two months went by and I was getting ready to go to trial for the kidnapping and car jacking charges. The day of trial I had been fasting to the Lord. I was dressed in a suit as I went in before the Judge to start trial. I went in and sat beside my lawyer Miss Patty. She told me not to say anything and that she would take care of everything. To my surprise everything took 30 minutes. I was found not guilty of the kidnapping and car jacking charges.

I praised the Lord all the way back to my cell. When I entered the cell block, all of my brothers in the Lord had been waiting on me because while I was at court they too had been praying for me. As I entered the cell block with a smile on my face. Everyone that saw me knew then and there that the Lord had made away for me. Now I had to face the other charges. (My lawyer told me that all of these charges had taking place on 8/3/2007). I continued to have service in the cell with the many people that would come. Those that came prayed and cried out to the Lord for forgiveness of their sins. As months passed many people were being added to the service that we would have together. The Lord was moving in a mighty way at the service in that jail house. I begin to pray and fast for the trial that was coming up. My faith was high in the Lord. I wasn't worried, I kept telling myself to trust in the Lord no matter how the trial may turn out. Many of the people would ask me, what if I go to prison. I said, "to them, if I go I'm going with the Lord in the name of Jesus. Many people that came to the service and gave their life to the Lord. I saw the mercy of God take place when they would go to court. Many charges were being drop and we gave praises to the Lord each time that someone would come back from court. Those that came back from court that felt like they was not so blessed, I encourage them not to give up on the Lord because the Lord always know what he is doing even when we can't see it. My next trial came around and I had been fasting that day as well. I entered the court room and sat down by my lawyer with my bible in my hand. I placed the bible on the table in front of me I then open the bible and began reading to myself. My lawyer told me to close my bible so I did. Trial began and ended in a blank of a eye. I was sick to my stomach. The jury had found me guilty. I couldn't believe my ears. I was so upset. The officer took me back to my cell. As I entered, many people that I had service with had a lot of hope in there eyes, but when they looked into my eyes, they knew then that I felt defeated but I didn't give up my faith. I knew that I was headed to prison. I never been to prison before but I didn't let that worry me because my trust was in the Lord no matter what. He is all I had before anyone thought to write me or send me money for canteen. Through it all the Lord had never left me but I have left the Lord many times when I turned to a life style of sin. I am bless to be able to thank the Lord for his forgiveness. I waited as two weeks passed by, I waited for sentencing day. The day that the Judge would sentence me to time in prison. I slowed down on the service and put more of my devotion toward the Lord.

CHAPTER 7

SENTENCING DAY

GALATIANS 6 7.

Be not deceived God is not mocked: for whatsoever a man soweth, that shall he also reap. Today was sentencing day, I had prayed all that I could pray. Whatever was going to happened was going to happened. I had faith in the Lord, so it didn't matter to me anymore. (I knew now that I was going to prison). I was in a holding cell waiting to be seen by the Judge. Many others was also waiting to see the Judge as well. Many of the people were encourage by each other, some of the people in that cell didn't speak about anything as others entered the cell from being seen by the Judge on this sentenced day. Some of the people that was seeing the Judge ahead of me came back with a smile because they had gotten a small sentence and was very greatful. As others in the cell was greatful for them. Some of the people came back from seeing the Judge was heart broken and defeated. my name was called and I entered the court room with a officer by my side. I was standing up in front of the Judge. I looked around and was pleased to see my mother also in the court room. (weeks before the sentencing my mother had written a letter of mercy to the Judge).

The letter was written from my mother but to the Judge on my behalf. The Judge then ask me to state my name for the court. I said, "Love Forever." The Judge said, "before I imply sentencing would anyone like to speak. My mother spoke good on my behalf and than my lawyer that was appointed by the court also spoke. I ask the Judge if it was okay for me to speak. He allow me to speak. I ask the Judge before he sentence me, I ask him for mercy. I told the Judge and the court that I was greatly sorry for my life style of running in sin. There was no mercy in this Judge heart at all. This Judge heart was made of stone when it came down to sentencing me. The Judge said, "Mr. *Love Forever*, I sentence you to 27 and a half years I had been through so much. I had been in the county jail for over a year. I was ready to get it over with. As the Judge spoke, I still had faith and courage but when I turn and looked at my mother. My faith and courage was soon short lived when I looked at my mother with so much hurt and pain in her eyes, her tears began to slowly fall. I broke down as though I was a little child. Reality had just hit me as though I was hit by a hurricane. I was okay until I saw the hurt and pain that I had caused my mother, it was to much for me to bear. My tears continued to fall from my eyes all the way back to the county jail. They place me in a cell where heart broken and defeated people are place to determine their state of mind, to be sure that the person doesn't try to kill his/her self. Heart broken, I met a guy that was also in the cell with me. He said, "are you okay man?," I looked up with tears in my eyes and said, "the Judge just gave me 27 and a half years." I couldn't stop the tears. I was crying for all the pain that I put my love ones through, I was crying for the people that I wouldn't see no more, I was crying for the friends and family that wouldn't be living if I had to do all of this time, I was crying because I had let my kids down and left them out there in a cold world without their father,. I was crying for the sorrow of my sins that had just caught up with me. The word of God is no lie whatsoever! truly you reap what you sow, I had been running in sin for so long. I prayed and cried, prayed and cried. The guy said, "don't feel bad, the Judge just gave me 19 years, I feel your pain bro. The only thing that I could think of was how could a Judge be so cold. I couldn't believe what just happened to me. A officer came to the cell and took me to a cell where I would be to myself, they took all of my clothes so I was in a cell naked with no bedding to lay on nothing but a concrete floor. They had camera's on me and they watch me. Some times a through the day a doctor would come to the cell and ask me if I was okay.

The first day and night in there I didn't speak to the doctor when he came through to talk to me and to see if I was okay. By the third day and night I told him that I was okay because I was tired of being in there. So they let me out and I went back to the cell block. I had stop doing the service but I would help people if they wanted to know something about the word of God. I would only share with them of what I learned from the word and hope that they would be helped from what was shared to them. I got up to use the bathroom and while I was doing a #2 I notice that I began to bleed again, just like I was when I was living on the out side of these prison walls. I put in to be seen by a doctor, he gave me the same medication that I received on the out side to help me with my bleeding. The bleeding went away just like it did when I was on the streets. Many people from the service that we would have had either got released or was blessed with a bond and had bonded out. Those that bonded out had left me with their canteen that they had left and wouldn't need because they was going back to their love ones and would be eating real food. I was greatful and shared some of the canteen that was left to me with other people. It didn't matter if they had been in the service or not, I was doing that in the name of the Lord. I was walking in the love of God even though I felt defeated.

PRISON EYES

CHAPTER 8

MY FIRST DAY IN PRISON

1 PETER 4 12-13

Beloved, think it not strange concerning the fiery trial which is to try you, as though some strange thing happened unto you:

But rejoice, inasmuch as ye are partakers of Christ's suffering

Two weeks later I was transfer from the county jail, many names where called. It was 2:30 am when the officers begin calling names. My name was called, the officer said, "*Love Forever*, pack your belongings. Some of the people that had been call was saying goodbye to their friends of whom they wouldn't be seeing in a very long time, some one said, "okay bro, I love you man, keep your head up, some one else that was sentence a little time at the county jail said, "be safe bro, I been there before you will make it. just stay to yourself bro, My Christian bothers said, "we got you in our prayers brother *Love Forever* be strong. I said, "I love y'all man keep the faith. This was the prison run day, many people that was call was ready to get it over with so that they could close this chapter of their life and get back to freedom because there was nothing fun about being in jail. The food was bad, they feed spoiled sandwiches a lot of times and you could find bugs in the food. Some times even mice were found in the breakfast. Their was a chance of catching scabies from the bedding and clothes that they gave us to wear. Living in jail was a nasty place to live in because of so many people that came in and out of the place, that you didn't know how they were living on the outside. It was by the grace of God that I made it through jail. I caught scabies twice since I been there and that is a very out of order feeling. Scabies is a little bug that you can not see that enter your skin and lay eggs everywhere inside of your skin and they bite you all day. They run up and down your skin. It is so bad that you would want to set yourself on fire to get rid of them.

As the officers place us in a holding cell. We waited for a hour and a half and then we heard something sound like a soda can began to opened. We all heard it and someone said, "that's our ride. We loaded up on the bus. The bus pulled off and we all looked out the small of the window as much as we could see because it would be a long time before a lot of us on that bus saw freedom again. We all rode for a few hours until we arrived at our destination. The bus pulled up to the prison and someone on the bus said, "here we go guys. I laid hold to my faith in the Lord no matter how this thing would turn out, it was a done deal. I was sentence to prison at the age of 27 years old with the sentence of 27 and a half years. As the bus stopped, we got our belongings in order and the door of the bus open. As soon as it open a officer that work at the prison ran to the doors of the bus and entered the bus yelling. He said, "you are now in my world! you don't speak! or eat! unless I tell you. Any one that breaks the rules, we will show you how we deal with them! (I thought to myself I said O Lord here we go) The officer said, "everybody off the bus! now! I want everybody to stand over here in a straight line no talking! Listen up closely. I want everyone to take off your clothes and put them in front of you. (Everybody did as they were told) He then said, "I want you to take off your finger and rub it in the inside of your mouth! now take your balls and lift them up! now I want you to bend over and spread your butt! (I said to myself, what kind of mess is this these people are crazy) One thing about being a Christian in prison is not only are you suffering for the Lord but you are also being punished. So it feels harder because it feels like a double punishment have been placed. After we was naked and search, We was allowed to put our clothes back on and then we had our belongings search and we had to go through the metal device to be sure no one was hiding any metal on their body. They gave us a small paper that told us what dorm we was in, I remembered the sign out front that said that I was at Holmes C. I. I headed to my dorm, I was a sign to F - dorm. It was a opened bay dorm where everyone Berri was in one big dorm, their was very little privacy. Every ones bunk was right next to each other (very close) If you laid on the bunk to sleep one way or the other way there was always a stranger that you didn't know that you would see. Their was always a person that didn't sleep as much. That person would stay up all night and if you looked over at the person, you would notice that person watching you. That person would be looking right at you. I stayed in opened bay for a month and then I was moved to a two man cell where I was behind a door and only two men was a sign to that cell. Only two men could stay there because there was only to bunks in each two men cell. (Many people some times wonder what or how prison is like, I always tell them if they want to know what/how prison is like, go into your bathroom and close the door that is how prison is like) I spent three months at Holmes C. I. I had seen so much violence and hatefulness. I never seen so much in my life. People were getting beating by other inmates. Some were getting their canteen took or stolen.

When I got in the two man cell which was H-dorm. When the officer would call for canteen. I would wonder why, that when most of the inmates came back from canteen, I would wonder why they would only buy two or maybe three items. They would use what they brought right then and there at that moment. One day I spent 30 dollars, I had put everything in my locker box and had locked it. The meal for that day was chicken. That's the day that everyone come close to eating real food because most of the meals are trash and I mean that. They have stuff on the tray that you don't even know the name of it or never seen in your life. Some of the food on the tray look like a eye ball blank at you. Many people have gotten sick from the food or the food would either mess your stomach up bad.

As I was locking my canteen food up. I heard the officer call for chaw. I went out the door and got in the chaw hall line. I went inside the chaw hall and ate what I could off the chicken that was cooked. When I went back to the dorm and went inside my cell. Everything looked fine. I got on my bunk and started reading my bible. My cellmate said a few words to me but I didn't trust him. I put my bible down and went to open my locker box to get my radio to listen to. When I open my locker, I couldn't believe my eyes. All of my canteen was gone. Someone had came in my cell while I was at the chaw hall eating and stole my canteen and radio. I was so mad, for a moment, I had forgotten all about the word of God. I was ready to fight. (I said to myself, my mother work to hard for someone to just come in my cell and take my belongings) They took everything but my legal work. I ask my cellmate did he see or know anything about my belongings being stolen. He said he didn't, but there was a funny look in his eyes. (it also came to my mind that most of his friends were doing all the stilling and things) I went to the officer and ask him did he see anybody come by my cell while I was at the chaw hall. The officer had seen someone but he couldn't remember who he saw. So we went from locker box to locker box in the dorm looking for my belongings. I was so mad that I started making threats and the officer lock me up (sent me to the box for making threats about my belongings) The box is another dorm but still part of the prison. A dorm where they place inmates when they get out of order. The box remind me of being in the county jail. It was very filthy and nasty and you took a chance of catching scabies as well. Their would be rat's running around the place at night in the cell. I'd the officer didn't like you he would be sure to have food missing from your tray doing feeding time. Some officers would even piss in the drinks that they would serve to the inmates that they hated. I sat back there in the box until I saw the Warden who then had me transfer to another prison 2 mons later. I arrived at Century C. I. I stayed there for four and a half years. When I got ere I went through the whole search thing again and I was given a paper to where my cell would be. One thing about prison is hoping for a good cellmate. I enter my new cell and told my new cellmate my name, he told me his name. Most cellmates start off okay but over time the real person always comes out. He was a coffee drinker. He love to drink coffee and smoke his tobacco. I didn't care for coffee at all. I had a bad experience from drinking coffee and after a time, smoking tobacco.

One day I drunk some coffee, I had been drinking coffee through out the day. Only cups of coffee, by night fall I couldn't sleep. My heart was beating so fast. I told myself never again, I'm through with coffee.

My cellmate was okay but he began to let his problems show. He began to take his emotions and anger out on other people. I had to deal with it the most because I was living in the same cell as he were. I also had my problems to deal with but I kept my problems to myself. I never took it out on anyone. I just prayed and dealt with it the best way I knew how to deal with it

It was 2010 when I first arrived at Century C.I.

My cellmate was getting worse by the day and even more worse by the night. I shared the word of God with him but his belief wasn't about Jesus Christ. It was about a high power that he believed in. So I let him believe what he wanted, it was his choice and his will. I stopped sharing the Lord Jesus Christ with him because it would turn into a argument. He slept at the top bunk, I slept at the bottom bunk. When he would get off the top bunk, he would be sure to stump his feet on the bottom bunk on purpose to try and get me to join his troubled mind but I wouldn't say anything.

One morning I was fed up with his additude. I had just come back from the chaw hall from eating breakfast. As soon as I pull the cell door up, but not closed, just up some to block out the noise so that I could go back to sleep. My cellmate put his hand in the door way and pulled the cell door back hard and fast and then he walked off. I jumped up from my bunk and went toward him, before it was said and done. I found myself sitting with my knee's in his chest with 3 inmates holding the arm that I was going to punch him with while he was on the ground on his back in a sorrowful motion. Other inmates broke it up before it got started and my cellmate and I sat and talked it out. We were trying to move to a different cell from each other. We talked to the officer about it and they didn't give us no kind of help. As the months went by my cellmate and I became good friends, he no longer took his anger out on me and I kept him in prayer.

CHAPTER 9

2 CORINTHIANS 6 16

And what agreement hath the temple of God with idols?
For ye are the temple of the living God

I continued to read and study my bible everyday but I knew I could have been doing better because I was smoking cigarettes. I had been trying to quit, but every time I tried the devil would be there to keep me from quitting. One day I said to myself, this is it, this is my last cigarette. Just as soon as I said that. A inmate came walking toward me and open his hand and laid six cigarettes down. He said, "here you go *Love Forever*, this is for you. I knew that it was the working of the devil because the Lord knew that I was his temple and that I was living for him and I really needed to stop smoking those cigarettes. Every time a problem would come up that I couldn't deal with. I would smoke a cigarette. I knew it was wrong because by being a Christian I was putting those cigarettes before the Lord when a problem would come up, instead of praying about the situation. I would smoke and I would feel the convection every time but I couldn't stop smoking. Those cigarettes became my idol. They became a God without me even realizing it. I had to quit, I had went from three cigarettes a day to one a day.

One morning the officer in the dorm call for rec. Rec is a time where inmates get to go outside and get some fresh air or get your workout on or just to feel a little freedom.

A older guy that I knew ask me did I want to go jogging, I said, "yeah." This older guy was okay to talk to, he had been doing time for a long time.

While I was getting ready for rec, I had just finish reading my bible and I fired up a cigarette, that was the only one that I smoked that day. As soon as I got finished smoking the cigarette. I felt the conviction I begin to pray. I said, "Lord please take this taste out of my mouth, help me Lord, I want to stop smoking cigarettes. I got up from praying and went to rec. (Now, keep in mind that when the Lord take something away from you when ask, the way he may take it away you may not like it but the job will be done. So as we go out side to rec. The older guy had another friend with him that wanted to jog with us as well. He looked at and his friend and said, "we are going to jog up this track, but when we turn around we are going to run back. I said, "okay." (I thought to myself, I can out run these old guys) We started jogging and when we got to the end of the track. They started running back down the way that they came. As they was running they looked around for me. They had left me and didn't know it because I wasn't running. I couldn't run, just from jogging that little jog, I couldn't catch my breath. My heart was beating to fast. The older guys turned around and came back for me. When they saw that I was having trouble catching my breath. They put one off my arms on each of their shoulders and help me to stand up. Another older guy that was across the track said, "I know what that is young blood, it's those cigarettes, they did me like that." Right then and there, I made my mind up that I was done with smoking. I said, "never again." I knew the Lord had took smoking away from me. Their was no more going back and forward with smoking cigarettes. I was done, and I knew it and I gave thanks to the Lord. Some times when others smoke cigarettes, and I could smell it, my heart would speed up a little. It was like the Lord was reminding me of that bad feeling that I experience. Never again did I ever want to experience that feeling nor did I ever want a cigarette.

As time went by I begin to work out and my health got better. I was able to run or jog with no problems.

Doing my 4 and a half years at Century C. I., my mother would visit me as well as my oldest brother (Plook). My youngest brother would at times visit on his own time because we have different mother but same dad. My youngest brother name is B. Forever He has been by my side along with my mother every since I came to prison. My oldest brother (Plook) soon began fading away from visiting me, sending me letters or money for canteen. He soon started working for F.D.O.C. I truly thank the Lord for my mother (*"Sincerely yours"* and for my brother Brian) They never left my side.

Century C. I. was the hottest prison that I had ever been to and the most violent prison that I had ever been too as well. The roof of that building was built with a tin roof, when the sun would heat up and shine on the roof of the building, it gets very hot and I mean super hot.

Their is no A/c or no kind of cool air that flows through the building in the summer time. When that tin roof heats up, the heat runs down the wall that's inside the cells and it's none stop heat until the next day early morning before the heat starts all over again.

One day I was in the cell with my cellmate and it was getting close to night fall. That cell was so hot from the sun shining on the tin roof. Every time the sun would shine on the roof, the heat from the sun would run down the walls of the prison cells like electricity and when the cells doors were close at night, there was getting no cold water to drink. The water that came out the sink would be hot to the taste

When night fall came, the cell doors were close for the night. My cellmate and I sweated dearly. We couldn't sleep, the sweat continued to pour out from our flesh and would burn our eyes. The electricity from the sun had saddled in the walls for the night and wasn't going anywhere soon. It was 3:45 am, neither my cellmate or I had slept.

Suddenly my cellmate started having trouble with he's breathing. He was having asthma attack and his inhaler was empty. I said, bunkie what you want me to do because if you want I will start kicking on the door for help?" He said, "just wait a second because it's close to 4:00 am, and they should be opening up the cell doors in a minute. A minute seemed like a hour and he was getting worse. I said, "bunkie, I'm going to start beating I and kicking the door for help. Suddenly the Lord saw the situation and made away because, out of 80 or more cell doors that was closed, our cell door open right before I started kicking on the door for help. Our cell door open before any cell door was open and nobody knew what was going on but the Lord and my bunkie and I. I helped my bunkie out the cell door and down the stairs and out another door to get to the officer station. We told him What was going on and another inmate saw what was happening and came out of the dorm from the other side of the officer station from another dorm. This inmate had his asthma inhaler in his hand and gave it to my bunkie to use until the nurse got there from the call the officer had made. Slowly but surely my bunkie went back to breathing normal again. I gave thanks to the Lord for my cellmate. As long as I could remember every summer of the four years and a half that I was there was super hot. It was hot in the summer time and cold in the winter time. There was always violence taking place in prison. The worse I seen yet, is when a inmate almost lost most of his nose.

One evening it was quiet, all of a sudden, you could hear inmates having a argument. It was a younger inmate and a older inmate. The younger inmate was standing in the door way of the older inmate cell door. The younger inmate said, "where is my money." because for some wicked reason the older inmate had played the younger inmate out of some money. The older inmate said, "I got your money right here, as the older inmate walked into the back of his cell. He reach under his bunk and with quick motion, the older inmate spends around with a razor blade sticking out of a toothbrush in his hand and slice the younger inmate across the nose. His nose folded down as though some one was pilling a potato. (I said to myself Lord have mercy) They began fighting like never before. The older inmate some how drops the razor blade while they were fighting. The younger inmate picks the razor blade up and starts using it on the older inmate. The younger inmate soon and slowly remove his self from the fight because he can't see. It's so much blood on his face and in his eyes. He look like he has been shot in the face with a shotgun. It's blood everywhere, all over the cell. As he removes his self from the fight. The officers that was called by the officer in the office station moves in to stop the fight. When they get there both inmates are cover in blood the two officers put hand cuffs on then and take them to the box. They walk by with the younger inmate, he has so much blood on his face that you couldn't even tell where the wound begin.

CHAPTER 10

ECCLESIASTES 3 1-8

To everything there is a season, and
a time to every purpose under the heaven.......
A time to love, and a time to hate a
time of war, and a time of peace.

There are so many different religions in prison. I kept to myself and I only
share the word of the Lord when I was moved by the Holy Spirit.

There are religions that I never hear of or about until I came to prison.
I knew that all these religions wasn't the truth because the word of the
Lord showed me so.

I would fellowship with those that were of the body of Christ and I
would witness to others that didn't believe anything. Being a Christian in
prison is a very hard walk. I had, and have to be ready for anything that
the devil may bring my way.

One night I was using the prison phone that was on the wall. There
were three of them on the wall and most of the time the phones were always
full. Doing this time there was a inmates in the dorm making trouble for a
lot of other inmates. Some of the inmates were either afraid of him or just
didn't want to get into any trouble because if you got into any trouble while
having a transfer in, the prison officials could have your transfer canceled.
Many inmates wanted their transfer because a transfer will send you to
a prison close to your family, only if the inmates put a transfer in to get
closer to their family. Either way nobody wanted to mess up their transfer.

While I'm on the prison phone, I was talking to my mother and my heart goes out to her because I could hear through the phone that she was in tears. As the lady comes on the phone to tell us that we got one minute left. My mother tells me to call her right back. Nobody said that they had next on the phone that I was using so, just as soon as I hang the phone up with my mother and redial her number. A inmate that was causing a lot of trouble in the dorm, in a wicked and forceful way, grabs the phone from my hand and tell me that he had next on the phone. When he grabs for the phone, the phone is still in my hand with my back turned to this trouble inmate. I turn around with the phone still in my hand and look at the trouble inmate in the eyes and said, "please man, don't do that, you don't know what's going on, on this end of the phone. With hatefulness in his heart and the devil having his way with this trouble inmate. He pulls on the phone that's in my hand. I pull the phone back and say, "please man you don't know what you doing. He pulls the phone back toward him. Now I have gotten angry because in my mind he was telling me that he didn't care of what was going on and he was not going to give me the respect that was due to me. So while he was pulling on the phone toward him. I said, "okay man you can have it, and with quick motion I let him have it, I punch him in the face in the head and arms. We broke off from each other with him saying, "this isn't over with." I told myself that I wasn't going to give him a chance to razor cut me or anything, we walked for about five minutes and he was yelling at me. He said, "this isn't over with, what's up. At that time a lot of inmates that I knew from Pensacola came out their cells to see what was going on. So the trouble inmate kept yelling and calling me to the fight. I went up toward him and he got in his fighting stand's. I just stud there looking at him, waiting on him to make the first move. He faked a punch and tried to grab me (big mistake) I wrapped my arms around his arms in a bear hug way and broke him down to the ground. I then let loose punches on him like a typewriter in a fast motion. He tried to stop my arms because I was on top of him in the fight. Doing the fight you could hear inmates yelling. One of his friends got to close to the fight as though he wanted to get a lick in on me because he didn't like the way that I was handling his friend. He shouldn't have never did that because someone from Pensacola attacked him for that. As I looked up. I saw a lot of people fighting. I looked around while I had the trouble inmate pinned to the ground. I looked toward the officer station to see if he was calling for backup because to many people had started fighting, the officer in the station kept reading his newspaper and turned his back on it all. Suddenly I put the troubled inmate in a death grip around his neck with my arms. I then began talking in his ear. I said, "what you want to do? I was angry but I didn't have the heart to kill him. He said, "I'm sorry. I said, "I was on the phone with my mother she was hurting you don't know what happened or who passed away, you just snatched the phone from me. He said, "I'm sorry. I tighten up my grip and said I know you sorry.

I soon let him go and went to ministering to him, I told him why do trouble come everywhere he goes. I told him to look at his self and seek for a change. He listen to me as I ministered to him. I told him that everything was okay between us and I also let him know that I had godly love for him. All the other fighting had also stopped. Either they got tired of fighting or they realize that if they wasn't going to kill anyone, than they needed to let go of the situation. The troubled inmate left the dorm. He told the officer that he couldn't be in that dorm anymore. So they took him out and placed him in the box. He was soon transfer. I never saw him again.

As months went by I continued to read and study my bible. I would go to the chapel once or twice doing the week. I would be sure to go on Sunday's because there would be a visitors up there ministering the word of the Lord, I enjoyed worship service. I was able then to get away from the dorm for awhile and be at peace while my mind was on the Lord as I listen to the songs of worship and praise. This was the only time that I felt free and felt the weight of prison, would be a little light from the everyday pain of missing love ones and friends. The rain from the dark cloud is removed only for a little while, until service ends and I have to return back to the dorm. A dorm filled with so much wickedness.

CHAPTER 11

GALATIANS 6 8

For he that soweth to his flesh shall
of the flesh reap corruption

Doing my time and stay at Century C. I., As the time went on I had different cellmates that I would call bunkies. I never was place back in open bay dorm and I was thankful for that because of the little privacy that I was able to have in the two man cell. Some of the bunkies I had stayed for weeks, others stayed for months and than they were transferred after a time. I had this one bunkie that I will never for get, because not only of the name he had but because he had a good heart. His first and last name is Harmon, and his last name is Herman. The first and last name sound the same. He was a very good bunkie, one of the best bunkies that I ever had. At that time both of us were into drawing pictures. We would do our time together in the cell away from the outside of the cell where a lot of foolishness took place. Harmon would help me through his family to look up long lost friends. One person I had him to look up for me, his family sent back the information by mail and I found out that she was married and had moved on with her life. I had him to look up another old friend of mines (Lisa) It took some time but we found her. I still remember the first phone call. I had used the prison phone one evening and I call and talk to my mother, doing the conversation with my mother I had told her about my ex girl friend Lisa and I ask her to call her on 3 way. My mother made the call and put me through. I'll never forget how, when I said, "hello, the moment Lisa heard my voice she couldn't stop screaming.

I said, "hello, Lisa. She continued to scream for 3 minutes. I was laughing with joy and smiling the whole time that she was screaming. A few weeks earlier, I had sent a letter to her from the information that Harmon had given me. I also received a letter back from her, but even then she couldn't believe it was me. As she stop screaming we began to talk and catch up on old times that we spent together. Weeks passed by and we kept in touch with each other. We would write each other every other day. I told her that I was save and that I was living for the Lord and she was cool with it and she began to work on herself because of the change in me that she had heard in my voice.

One day while using the bathroom, I being to bleed. So I went to the doctor and they put me in for a transfer to see a specialist. Two weeks later I was transferred to a hospital prison call Lake Butler.

Lake Butler Is a prison where they send inmates to when the problem or situation is out of the reach of the doctors, from which prison the inmate was housed at to do his time.

When I arrived at Lake Butler I stayed there for 3 months, just sitting there. When I finally seen the doctor. He explained to me that I had internal hemorrhoids. He sent me back with no treatment. When I got back to Century. I put in to see the doctor at Century. They gave me a treatment and the problem went away for a little while. I was thankful to be away from Lake Butler even though I was seeking for help. There was to many out of order things taking place there. The officers was beating on the inmates for the smallest things.

The officers at Lake Butler would beat a inmate if he looked up when a female officer walked by. Sometimes the male officers would let the female officers beat on a inmate while the male officers watch.

When I entered Lake Butler for the first time. I saw this tall officer, he had to be 6, 2 and weighed 310 pounds. I watched that officer knock fire from a inmate.

As I sat in intake with 40 other inmates. I heard and saw this white inmate ask this black inmate, the white inmate said to the black inmate, he said, "hey man, do you want to go in the bathroom with me and smoke? the black inmate said, "I'm good man, it don't look safe to be smoking in here." The White inmate turns to a Spanish inmate and said, "what's up man, you trying to go in the bathroom and smoke." The Spanish inmate said, "sure why not." While all the other inmates including my self was sitting down in the chairs. The white and Spanish inmate, gets up and walk over to the bathroom to smoke. While the 310 pounds officer was getting property in order. The Spanish inmate and the white inmate didn't notice that the officer was watching the big mirror that hangs at the corner wall of the bathroom were he could watch the bathroom while he gets the inmates property in order. Before the white inmate could lite the cigarette up. The 310 pounds officer was in the bathroom with them, the officer looks at the white inmate that was on the right of him, then he looks at the Spanish inmate. He then said, "while looking at the Spanish inmate, so y'all just going to smoke, is that right? suddenly while looking at the Spanish inmate with quick motion he slaps the White inmate, and then turns from the Spanish inmate and looks at the white inmate and repeats his self.

He said, "So y'all just going to smoke huhh? Suddenly with quick motion while looking and talking to the white Inmate he turns and slaps fire out the Spanish inmate as well, both of the inmates that was slapped by the 310 pounds officer, when he slapped them each at a time, each one of their heads and body did a spend around. When I saw that I was praying to the Lord to bless me to enter that place in peace and to leave that place in one peace. That was my first time seeing a officer put his hands on a inmate, and from the look of it I know it wasn't going to be the last.

While I'm back at Century, I had a good adjustment transfer in to be transfer away from that place. A good adjustment transfer is a transfer that you earn for staying out of trouble with no write ups. I had put my good adjustment transfer in to a prison call Blackwater, that prison had just open up. It was a private prison. A prison at the time for inmates who like to do easy time.

One day while talking on the phone to my mother, I explained to her that I would be leaving soon and that I would be going to Blackwater. I was so happy to be getting away from Century, I couldn't wait to leave. My mother gave me some unkind news. She told me that my brother (Plook) my oldest brother had started working for the prisons and his paper work was put in for Blackwater prison or either Century where I was located. I told my mother that I had a bad feeling. I said, "well, I hope he come to Century because I'm trying to go to Blackwater. My mother said, "let's wait and hope and see what happens son." We finished our conversation and I would always be sure to thank her and tell her that I love her for standing by my side all these years.

A month had passed by and I was in my cell playing a chest game with my bunkie, Harmon when my name was call to report to the officer station. As I go to the officer station, the officer had told me to pack my belongings because I was being transferred. I went back to my cell and started packing my things and to tell Harmon that I was leaving. He was happy for me but I was sad for him because I wish that he would have been transferring as well.

Century was not a place for a change man to do time, troubled was everywhere and everyday someone got stabbed, everyday, and there was always a fight, everyday.

The only good days I had there was when I went to church or stayed in my cell other than that the place was always being locked down because of the fighting and stabbing and things.

I gave Harmon a hug and said goodbye to him as I walked out the dorm toward the bus. Many others wish me well as I left. I felt so bless to be leaving Century, a place of hell. When I would minister to the those that wasn't save,/I would always tell them that the next step is hell, and I would tell them that after hell you couldn't go any lower than that if they didn't get their life right with the Lord.

As I got on the bus and as we pulled away from Century, I knew that I was blessed. I enjoyed looking out the bus window at freedom. It was beautiful outside, it was a lovely day as the bus drove on, heading to Blackwater and other stops that needed to be made.

I arrived at Blackwater that same day. I got off the bus with other inmates and we were searched and sent to the dorm that we would be in, I call my mother and Lisa when I got there and told them that I had arrived. This prison was a lot better than Century. They had cool air! I was so thankful of the Lord for that. I couldn't get enough of the cool air. My new cellmate was troubling. We wasn't cool at all, he couldn't understand that I didn't care about worldly things so we didn't see eye to eye the whole time that I was there. He wanted me to praise the naked picture he had and I told him that I didn't care about those worldly things. So he would be mad at me because I didn't agree with his mind set. One day while talking on the phone with my mother, she surprised me and told me that Lisa would be coming down to see me. Lisa stayed out of town. Lisa was the only girlfriend that my mother ever liked. She was crazy about Lisa, my mother told me that Lisa would be staying with her while she was down her. They would talk and get to know each other, when I wasn't talking to either of them on the phone. They became close, two weeks later Lisa was down here in Pensacola at my mother house. I was happy I couldn't stop smiling, knowing that I would soon see Lisa because Lisa and my mother was coming for a visit. That weekend they came, it was my mother and her husband and Lisa. It had been so long since I held a woman of my heart.

My name was called for my visit and I left the dorm and entered the visitation dorm. I sat down and waited and then suddenly I saw my mother walking in with Lisa and my mother husband. I hug my mother and give her a kiss and then I hug Kenny and turn to Lisa.

The whole time while I was hugging my mother and Kenny, I'm watching Lisa with the look in her eyes that's saying hurry up I want my hug and kiss now! She looked so beautiful. I soon hug Lisa and sat at the table and talked. My mother told Lisa that Kenny and her would be back later to pick her up when visitation was over. They left as to be and Lisa and I caught up on old times, we talked, took picture, laughed. She cried and then the visitation was over. Lisa return the next day, visited, of that Sunday of that weekend. We talked, ate, and took more pictures. It was lovely to be away from the dorm. That first hug from her was like heaven. I could have died right then and their and I would have been okay. I told her that and she started laughing and said, "boy you so silly. When the visit ended we hugged and kissed and I went back to the dorm.

I call my mother and talk to her and then she gave the phone to Lisa.

Lisa took the bus back home and I would call and check on her as she rode the bus home.

One night doing count time (count time is when every inmate is in his cell and sitting on the bunk being counted) I saw my oldest brother walking through. He was in training by another officer. I couldn't believe my eyes. I saw him but he didn't see me. I knew for sure that I was going to get transferred. I said, "dang! I then call my mother and told her when count was cleared. Two days later as I was coming in the dorm from the rec yard. A lady officer walked up to me and said, "are you Love Forever? I said, "yes ma'am." She said, "turn around and cuff up. She took me to the box. Blackwater box was much cleaner and much safer. They also had a phone that I never seen.

This phone was on a stand with a cord that came from the back of the phone so that it could be plugged up in to the wall. There were also wheels on this stand so that the officer could rolled the phone from cell to cell. That was the first time that I ever seen something like that. A officer came by my cell door and I ask him why was I back here in the box. He said, "because your family member works here so we have to transfer you out.

I had two cellmates while I was back there and I ministered to each of them as one came and one left in the two man cell. I was able to call and talk to my mother. I explained to her the situation and that, I would be transferring.

I sat back there for two and a half months and than I was transferred. I was sent to another prison, it was called Santa Rosa, that prison was only five minutes away from Blackwater, and Blackwater was only ten minutes away from Pensacola. So I wasn't far from home, on the other hand, when I was at Century, that place was a hour and 30 minutes away.

I arrived at Santa Rosa and went through the search thing again and I was handed a paper to where my cell would be. As I got to the dorm and entered my cell, there was a guy name Mike in there, he was my new bunkie. Mike and I got along fine. While Mike and I was putting up our belongings, some black guy came to the cell to make trouble with Mike.

Mike had a look of fear in his eyes as he held on to his bible. I ask Mike was he in the word and he said he were. Mike then told me that the back guy that was troubling him also had three more friends that was on this guy side. The words of the Lord ran through my heart at that moment while mike was explaining the situation to me (2 TIMOTHY 1; 7 For God hath not given is the spirit of fear; but of power, love, and of a sound mind. ROMANS 8; 15 For ye have not received the spirit of bondage again to fear;) When the guy came back with another guy. I told them to trouble somebody else because I wasn't going to let them trouble my new bunkie Mike. They left and I told Mike to grab his lock and be ready to use it if they come back. I knew that Mike wasn't no fighter and I wasn't going to stand there and watch those guys put their had on Mike. They never came back to that cell and they never bothered Mike again. Three weeks later that guy that was troubling Mike had got his self into some trouble that he couldn't handle He got beat so bad that he ran to the box (confinement) As weeks went by I begin to talk to Lisa on the phone, things wasn't going good with our relationship. She didn't want change for the better. She continued to live in her old ways. Every time I would call her and bring up the name of the Lord, she would begin to get hateful. She had stopped allowing me to witness to her. She would hang up the phone on me.

One day we had gotten into a argument on the phone. I hung the phone up and let it go. I knew that as long as she live a sinful life style that we wouldn't work out. She was going one way and I was going another. It was just like I had studied in the word off God, about light and darkness. You can not put the two together because if you go into a dark room and turn on the light, than you want see the darkness anymore just as well as you go into a room of light and you turn the light off, you can not put the two together and that is what was taking place with Lisa and I, that is what was taking place with our relationship. (CORINTHIANS 6;14-18

Be ye not unequally yoked together with unbelievers:

for what fellowship hath righteousness with unrighteousness? and what communion hath light with darkness?.....

17. Wherefores come out from among them, and be ye separate, saith the Lord.

As months begin to take place, I begin to bleed again while using the bathroom. I put in to see the doctor and he gave me the same medication that didn't work. The bleeding begin to get worse.

The doctor ran a few more test and than he realized that I needed to be seen by a specialist. I was put in for a transfer back to Lake Butler. I went back to the dorm and call my mother and explained to her of what was taking place. I stayed in prayer because at this point of my life of loosing so much blood. I didn't know if I would live or die, so I continued to pray. I also told Mike my situation because we became very good friends. I also would attend service that they had at the chapel through the week and on Sundays. I would go up there and sign the little prayer box that was up there where inmates could write down their need of prayer.

Santa Rosa had the best chapel out of all the prison that I ever been to. I was well please to enjoy the word of the Lord there. Many inmates were being save and everything was ran in order. The Lord was surely in that chapel. Though I was in another prison with cool air, the violence was at it highest, inmates were being stab every day or getting hit in the head with a lock or getting hurt while they were sleeping, but praise the Lord, He kept me safe.

CHAPTER 12

MARK 8 34-35

And when he had called the people unto him with his disciples also, he said unto them, whosoever will come after
me, let him deny himself, and take up his cross, and follow me
For whosoever will save his life shall lose it but whosoever
shall lose his life for my sake and the gospel's, the same shall save it.

Three weeks later I was transferred to Lake Butler. I was search and given my little paper to tell what dorm I was going to. Lake Butler is one of the oldest prisons ever built. I entered a building called I block, it was a very old place. There were lots of birds flying around in the place and a lot of windows that were broken and no one cared about fixing the windows.

When I got there, I notice a lot of inmates with bad health problems just as before but with more inmates. Some of the inmates were passing away right before your eyes, left and right everywhere you looked from their health issues. The doctor would tell some of the inmates how long they had left to live. I seen a lot of different kinds off sickness. I met a few inmates that I did time with that was there for a health problem. As weeks and months went by, I begin to see the specialist but they wasn't doing much of nothing for me. I continued to pray and fast while I was there and I continued to loose a lot of blood. I was loosing cups full of blood every time that I would use the bathroom and do a #2. I thought for sure that I was dying or was going to die because this problem had been going on for years off and on but now it has got to the point where the problem didn't want to go away. The officers there was different, they would reward you if kept the dorm cleaned up. They would bring in food and share it with you. The job that

I had was passing out the blues (clothes) to all the inmates in the dorm. I would make sure that everyone got the right size clothing. The officer was well please because it made him look good in front of his boss, it showed that the officer in charge was running the dorm the right way. Every Sunday at Lake Butler the officers would cook deer meat on the grill every Sunday that I was there. At times I would get a piece of that deer meat that they would cook, it was a blessing to taste real food for a change.

One morning I was surprise to see that the officer in charge cooking pancakes right there by the officer station. He had brought in one of those small skillets that you could make things on. He made pancakes for the officers he'd work with and I was surprise when he also made some for the four workers that was keeping the dorm clean.

There were very little Christian inmates or officers that I saw there. I ran into one Christian officer. It was crazy how we met, he was in the dorm and I had just came in the dorm from trying to get some canteen and as I came up the stairs and entered the dorm, he stopped me, He said, where you headed? I said, "I just came back from trying to find out was canteen opened, some of the officers didn't care off how many times that you would clean up they would let you go to the canteen window." He said, "next time you go down there without my permission I'm going to have my team come up here and beat you. I looked at him with the love of God in my eyes and said in a humble voice, I said, "Sir you will have me beat all because I was trying to get something to eat? Something must have touch him because he looked at me with sorrow in his eyes and said, "go head on, its okay. Every since than he would always make sure that I was okay and he would let me go to canteen any time that I wanted. I knew that the favour of the Lord was upon me, because he would even let me pick ten inmates to let me take them with me to canteen. The inmates that I picked would buy me items for taking them to canteen because if you didn't have no job at Lake Butler, a lot of times it was very hard to get to canteen. Weeks would go by and the officer that did the canteen call would skip right over the dorm that I was in (I block) but by me being a clean up man I was able to come and go as I was pleased and I was very greatful of the Lord for that.

I went back and forward to the doctor so they could run more tests. I would make sure to call my mom to let her know of what was going on. She would always tell me to stay prayed up.

When night fall came doing mail call. I had received a form from the specialist with instruction on the form telling me to report to the medication window. I was getting ready to take a (M.I.R.) It's a procedure that the specialist have done to determine the problem of ones health.

The next morning I go to the medication window to pick up the medication for the (M.I.R.). I pick up this gallon jug that has medication in it that I have to mix with water.

I go back to my cell and fill the jug up with water as the instruction states. I begin drinking this nasty stuff that make me want to throw up. I have to drink it to clean myself out so that when the doctor check me out I want have anything in my stomach. I cleaned myself out that whole day and I was also instructed not to eat anything until after the procedure. The next morning came and I was sent to were the doctors do the procedures. I had a I.V. placed in my arm and after. I was given a little pill to take. I was then sent in a private room. After a few minutes the specialist came in the room with a nurse that would help with the procedure. I laid in a bed on my stomach and the doctor put a camera up my butt and watched a small T. V. screen as he search with the camera to determined the problem. He soon found the issue and took pictures with the camera that he had running through me. When he was done he took the camera out and left me there for a few minutes to review the pictures. When he came back, he explained to me that I had internal hemorrhoids.

I leave the doctor with a slip from him to pick up medication. I go to the medication window and pick up my medication. I realize that it's the same meds that I had been receiving for years. (I said to myself I know this stuff isn't going to work. I have been trying this stuff for years) I go back to the dorm (I block) and don't know how to think, months are passing by and I'm still at Lake butler. (nothing hasn't change) My issue begin to get worse. I sat there and prayed. I began to feel pain from this issue that I was having along with the bleeding. I waited on the Lord to see what was going to be done about the situation. I called my mother and informed her on what was taking place and what has been done. I continued to work and keep my mind off of things but I was sad in the inside because nobody wrote me a letter to see how I was doing. Every since I left Blackwater, my oldest brother had stop writing me letters and sending me money for canteen. I didn't hear from nobody but my mother. I thanked God truly for my mother.

CHAPTER 13

MARK 5 25-34

And a certain woman, which had an
issue of blood twelve years,
And suffered many things of
many physicians, and had spent all that
she had, and was nothing better, but
rather grew worse,
when she had heard of Jesus, came
in the press behind, and touched his
garment.
For she said, if I may touch but his
clothes, I shall be whole.
And straightway the fountain of her
blood was dried up and she felt in her
body that she was healed of that plague.....
And he said unto her, Daughter, thy
faith hath made thee whole go in peace
and be whole of thy plague.

I begin to think about what that woman was dealing with and the situation that I too was suffering. I prayed and ask the Lord to heal me just as he healed that woman in his word. I also thought about the fact that I had suffered just about the same amount of years as this woman had. I was tired of suffering from this, I knew that I was reaping what I sowed.

I also knew that the Lord mercy is great and I had faith that something's was going to take place for me, just as it was taking place for that woman. I continued to pray and have faith. I kept on working in the dorm to keep my mind off of things.

One morning as I was getting the clothes ready. The officer that cooked the pancakes walked up to me and said, "Hey *Love Forever* make sure they keep the noise down in the dorm and let me know if a white shirt come, I'm going to take a nap,"(I said to myself this is not my job) But I said, "okay anyway to him. It wasn't my plan to tell the dorm to do anything, but I didn't mine letting the officer in charge know when the white shirt would come. (The white shirt is the captain, but most people in prison call them White shirt because he wears a big white shirt).

A lot of inmates was hateful toward me. I could see it in there eyes, they didn't like the fact that I could go to canteen when I wanted to and eat deer meat and other real foods at times. So as I'm walking down the dorm doing some cleaning. I notice that it got to loud on the wing. I said out of love,/ I said, "hey man the officer said he will lock everyone down if it gets to loud. The guy looks at me in anger and said, "what you the police or something. I said, "be for real man, I'm just trying to help, so that he want lock y'all down. The troubled inmate and I, get into argument and then a fight. We are fighting a minute while I'm getting the best of him, his friend don't like it and come from behind me and hit me with a baby punch and then runs off. The officer in charge and another officer yells for us to stop. I move back away from the fight and put a knee on the ground to show the officer that I was listening. While I was backing off from the fight the officer rush the troubled inmate that I was fighting with and slammed him on his back, at the same time that this officer was slamming this troubled inmate. This same officer dislocated his arm and started screaming. The officer had cuffed me and the troubled inmate and took us to medical one by one. I went first (when a fight would happened, and finished with, when the officer hand cuffs a inmate, the inmate has to go to medical before he is placed in the box, confinement.) The officer that dislocated his arm also went to medical while the officer and I were in there, he's telling everybody that's in there that I'm a good person. He was screaming this out through his pain.

I was place in the box along with the troubled inmate but we were in different wings while we were in the box.

The next day I received a D. R. (A D. R. is a form that is given to a inmate that has gotten into trouble when a D. R. form is given, A inmate has to report to D.R. court to find out the out come of the D.R. report. If a inmate is found guilty of the D.R., than he/ she has to do more box time) I went to D.R. court two days later and they released me back to the dorm. The D.R. staffs had mercy on me because I was defending myself.

I went back to the dorm and continued to clean the dorm to pass time. The officers continued to bring me food. Sometimes they would offer me cigarettes but I would tell then I would rather have the food. The other inmates that were helpers of the dorm took the cigarettes with pleasure. As weeks went by I still haven't heard anything about getting help with my issue. I continued to have faith in the Lord that something was going to happened for the good. One morning while I was sleeping, I was waken by a loud screen, someone was yelling and screaming. It was coming from the officer station. I got up along with other inmates to see what was going on. As I got closer to the officer station I see four officers and one inmate. The inmate looked as though he weighed 110 pounds. He was laying on the ground while the four officer was stomping him with there boot's. I couldn't bear to see what was taking place, so I started yelling along with other inmates for them to stop. The officer in charge yelled back and told us to get back and go to our cell. Watching that take place troubled my heart. I couldn't let it go. I got on the phone and call the crime number that was place on the wall by the phone. It was a free number that any inmate could call. I called the number and reported the crime and gave names. I also wrote the warden and explained what had happened. The four officers that stomped on that inmate ended up getting in trouble. They got suspended from work for a few days. They was very angry about being suspended. They was so angry that they researched and found out that it was me that reported them. While they were suspended they called in their friend officers to retaliate against me and a inmate name T C.

One afternoon doing lunch time, I bock was called for lunch. For some reason the spirit of the Lord was place on my heart not to go to lunch. So I stayed back. I didn't go, five minutes later a officer came walking in the dorm looking at cell numbers. I was walking up and down the dorm talking to the Lord. I notice that the officer stopped at my cell. I just look at him to see what he was up to. He suddenly goes into my cell yelling and cursing while throwing all my belongings on the ground. I walk up to him and said, "Sir are you okay? He then looks at me with evil and hatefulness in his eyes and leave the dorm.

Doing this time their was cameras put up in the dorm because of so many reports that Lake butler was receiving. Someone higher up wanted to make sure that the officers wasn't mistreating the inmates.

I put in my paper work to the warden about that officer and I told the warden that I was suffering from retaliation because of the crime that I had reported. That officer got suspended also, but that didn't stop the retaliation.

The next day another officer call me to the officer station and ask me was I going to pass out the inmates clothes and put them in order. When I got finished with the clothes, I went to my cell, while my back was turned, he closed my cell door and told me to stay in e cell for that day. I also wrote him up and the next day there was a different officer working in the officer station. This officer did not cause trouble with me but more trouble was on the way. The next morning I woke up and spoke to T C, before we could get into a conversation, the officer that was in charge and had been suspended was back at work that morning. He walked up to my cell with another angry officer, T C cell was close by the cell that I was in, only ten feet apart. The officer in charge and the other officer that was with him walk up to me and said, "y'all need to start cleaning, scrubbing these windows, clean the floor, do this, do that. (Now keep in mind that I only cleaned from the kindness of my heart, I didn't have to clean, that wasn't the reason that I was at Lake butler). I was there for medical reasons only. I told both of the officers, I said, "Sir no disrespect, but I'm not here to clean, I'm here for medical reasons. At the same time that I was explaining this to the officer, T C said, I'm not cleaning up I'm here for medical. The officers told him as well as me to turn around and cuff up. As I turn around and cuffed up I continued to explain that I was there for medical. They took T C and I to the box and placed us In a holding cell together until they found a cell for us. They found a opened cell for T C first and then they came and took me to a cell a hour later. T C and I were in different cells, we couldn't speak to each other because he was on a different side of the box. I was so tired and frustrated. Nine months had passed and nothing was being done about my bleeding situation. I found myself getting into unwanted trouble. I was just tired of being there. I hadn't received a D.R, so I ask a officer that was walking by my closed cell door. I said, "Sir why I'm I back here." He said, "I will be right back, let me go find out. He comes back 45 minutes later and tell me that I'm under investigation for refusing to clean up. (I said to myself they are playing games with me). The officer also said that I made someone mad. I was back there for 14 days. They wouldn't give me no toothbrush, and no deodorant. I tried to clean myself up the best way that I could. I would take a bird bath in the sink because they wouldn't even allow me to take a shower. I was smelling bad I had to use toothpaste under my arms to keep the smell down and soon the toothpaste began eating the skin from underneath my arms. I had to stop using that for deodorant. While I was back there, my bunkie and I get into a argument and come close to fighting. I was frustrated from being back there and so was he. I stud up and walk toward him with the love of Jesus Christ in my eyes and said, "hey man, with tears in my eyes because of the love of God. I said, "if I have wrong you or did anything to you, please forgive me, I'm sorry. He couldn't believe what was taking place with me. He also had a look of sorrow in his eyes when he looked at me. He said, "I'm sorry too man, you was right about what you was saying, I do need to change, I don't know why I was trying to get you upset. I said, "everything okay God bless you man.

The next morning while I was a half of sleep I hear my name being called on the out side of the cell door. I looked up and see my bunkie standing by the door as the white shirt passed by the door, my bunkie said, "I think they are looking for you." My bunkie move away from the door and I jump down off the top bunk to see what was going on. The white shirt comes back to the cell door that I'm in and said, "are you *Love Forever*, I said, "yes Sir, in his hand was one of my report forms that I had written right before they put me in the box. He hold's the form up and said, "if I let you out to day can I get rid of this (he was talking about the report that I had written) I said, "yes Sir if you tell your officers to leave me alone." He said, "we are going to let you out today but I need you to come and see me when I let you out, as soon as you get out come and see me." I said. "yes Sir." They let me out and before I left the cell I told my bunkie that he would also be out soon. He told me that he would see me out there. I walked around the prison looking for the white shirt. One officer stop me and ask me where I was going, I told him that the captain told me to come and see him. The officer pointed me where the captain was located and I headed towards the chaw hall where he was standing, I walk up to him and said, "yes Sir you wanted to see me? He said, "that's right, is everything over with? (he was speaking about the reports that I had and the things that I knew about) I said, "yes Sir but I need you to tell your officers to leave me alone because I got more things written down that they did that you don't even know about." He said, "Mr. *Love Forever*, you don't have to worry about them no more." I said, "thank you Sir, with humbleness in my eyes and as I walked off, He said, "good day.

I made it back to I bock dorm and saw T C standing there. He was happy to see me just as well as I was happy to see him. He said. "you need something to eat because he knew that it was a great suffer to be in the box without no canteen and things. T C said, "I was waiting for you to get out, what happened? he said, that he had gotten out of the box a week before I got out. I told him that they just kept me there longer. As weeks went by I didn't have to worry about any officers bothering me anymore. I had no more problems with those troubling officers.

They had put the Christian officer in charge of I block dorm. I had the favour of the Lord on my side I was not only allowed to take Inmates from I block to canteen bug I was also allowed to go to D-dorm, C- dorm or any other dorm without so much as a officer stopping me asking me anything. Inmates loved me because I could get them to canteen when they couldn't get there. They loved me and I loved them because they made sure that if I got them to canteen, I didn't have to spend no canteen money.

CHAPTER 14

PHILIPPIANS 4 19

But my God shall supply all your need
according to his riches in glory by Christ Jesus.

Another day gone and another night had come.
I was in the dorm talking to one of my Christian brothers name Beline.
He was telling me about this church he went to for a month before he got
locked up. He told me how supported and nice and loving that the people
are at that church. He also told me how they always keep in touch with
him and he felt bless because he only been there for a month. I went to
thinking about the church that I was attending, when I was on the outside
and I became sad. I thought about the letters I had written to the church
over the years, and haven't received any letters back in return. My heart is
broken from the thought, even until this day. I knew that my letters had
been received because I would write my baby brother Brian there, and he
would get my letters every time. I soon dismissed the thought because my
name was called for mail call. I had received a form to report to the surgeon
doctor. I knew then that the Lord was getting ready to move on my behalf.

The next day I went to talk to the surgeon doctor, he ask me some
question and then he said, "I'm going to run some test, and if I see that
you are bleeding we are going to have surgery. (I said, "to myself, showing
you the blood that I been loosing want be no problem at all)

He ran some tests and seen that I was loosing a lot of blood. I was to
report to him the next day. I reported to him and he told me that I was in
luck, but I knew that it was the Lord. After my conversation with him. I

left his office feeling bless because he told me that tomorrow he would have me in for surgery. I gave thanks to the Lord and went to the medication window to pick up the meds to clean myself out for the surgery. I clean myself out all that day and night. I got on the phone to tell my mother the good news. I told her that they would be putting me to sleep doing the surgery. I told her that some people died in there sleep doing surgery. She encouraged me not to worry about it, She said, "son just ask the Lord to forgive you of all your sins and just go through with it and than you will feel better and be ready if something were to happened, I believe that you are going to be okay son." My mother made me feel strong to go through this without being afraid.

I prayed that night and went to sleep. I got up the next morning and my name was called to head on over to the surgery station. When I got there, other inmates were also waiting for surgery as well because of the issues that they was dealing with. While I was waiting, I hear a woman in one of the surgery rooms screaming in so much pain. My heart started beating fast. I begin to pray.

My name was call and they put me in a bed with a I.V. in my arm. When the I.V. was finished they took me Into one of the surgery rooms. They then lifted me off the bed and put me on a surgery table that was shape like a cross. They took my arms and put them on each side of the cross like table. They then strapped my arm in to the cross like surgery table. The surgery doctor then put a mask over my face that held sleeping gas. When he put the mask on my face I started repenting for all my sins. When I had finished praying for the Lord to forgive me. The doctor told me to count backwards to ten. I said 10, 9, 8, was the last number that I remembered. I was out like a light. I don't know how long that I was out but I was waken up by the doctor and He said, "we are all done." (I said to myself, man that was fast) I didn't feel anything doing the surgery. They rolled me down on the bed to the recovering room. I laid there for 20 minutes and then I started feeling pain back there. I started yelling and then a nurse came and gave me some pain pills that was ordered by the doctor. Suddenly I had to pee I had to do a # one so I slowly got out the bed and walked pass other inmates that was recovering. I made it to the bathroom but nothing would come out. (I said to myself what is going on, what have they done to me) I slowly walked in the hallway to get help.

I saw a nurse walking around in the hallway. I stopped her and told her that I needed help. I told her that I couldn't use the bathroom. She went and returned with another nurse. They had me to remove my surgery clothing that I had on. They then put a tube inside my sex drive. The tube was connected to a bag. Just as soon as the tube was inside of me. I started peeing (doing a number one) I didn't even know that I was peeing. I looked at the nurse, I said, "did anything come out? She said, "yes, you just about filled the bag up. I looked down at the bag and surely the bag was almost filled.

As days and weeks passed by, I begin to heal. I was giving thanks to the Lord because I was ready to leave Lake butler.

Summer time was around the corner and these big roaches was coming out and crawling in everyone's cell. These roaches would be everywhere and they would crawl over you while you were trying to sleep. It was hard to sleep doing that season. I have never seen anything like it you would kill one and 30 minutes later, the one that you killed is being eating by the other roaches. I have seen roaches before but these roaches look like baby mice.

The reason it was hard to sleeping also was because of the loud noise of the stumping and slapping of the locker box of every time someone's tried to kill a roach. This would go on all night until morning. For some reason these things came out at night, and when the sun came up, these things would vanish.

One night doing mail call. I had received my license. Before I left Santa Rosa, and came to Lake butler. I had been studying the word of God for a license. I was surprised to receive this mail at Lake butler because I was taking the course at Santa Rosa. I was so happy and my brothers in the Lord was happy for me as well. My faith had went to a much higher level with the Lord and it wasn't just because of the minister license I had received. It was because the Lord had healed me from death. I was and I am still very greatful of what the Lord has did in my life and of what he is still doing. I believe with all my heart that the word of God is real and true.

CHAPTER 15

PSALM 103 1-4

Bless the Lord, o my soul: and all that
is within me, bless his holy name.
Bless the Lord, o my soul, and forget
not all his benefits:
Who forgiveth all thine iniquities
Who healeth all thy diseases
Who redeemeth thy life from destruction

I begin to heal very well as the days passed by. I would stop and fellowship
with the Christians brothers, T C and I had became very close friends.
What brought us close was the word of the Lord and the suffering we went
through while we was there.

The next morning while it was still dark out. My name was call by
a officer that had a list in his hands. It was a transfer list. It was time for
me to go back to Santa Rosa. I had been here and the Lord had bless me
to have surgery. He had healed me and I was ready to go. I didn't want
no more parts of Lake butler. I packed up my belongings and stop by T
C cell. I told him that I was out. He said, "I see that you beat me out of
here." I said, "yes I did." He gave me his address because he was a short
timer (a person that didn't get sentence with a lot of time) I said, "God
bless you bro and he said the same." I left and got on the bus. The bus ride
was lovely. I was able to see freedom and kept my hopes up until the Lord
bless me out of prison.

It was the year of 2016.

I had just arrived back at Santa Rosa, I got off the bus as well as other inmates that had been transferred there. We was search and given a piece of paper for the location of the dorm. As I'm walking to the dorm, I see some of my Christian brothers. I was so happy and bless to see them. It was a joyful feeling. I haven't seen those guys in a year, and they haven't seen me in a year. Some of the brothers knew my situation and knew why I was transferred to Lake butler. I saw my good friends and brothers in the Lord, my brother Mark said, "hey brother *Love Forever*, look at me I got hair and then he points to his head. I said, "I see and we started laughing and gave each other a hug as well as the other brothers that was standing around while we talked for a minute.

I make it to my cell and speak to my new bunkie. He's a order guy that has been in prison for 25 years. We get along fine. He knows how to do time peacefully. As weeks pass by I am surprise to see that my ex wife Kim have got in touch with me. She writes me and I write her back. She explained to me that she had remarried but the guy she married had came home one day while Kim was at work and packed up his things and had left her. (I thought to myself, well maybe she is reaping what she sow, because I remember after we was married, the next day she was gone). I ask her what had happened that night of the next day when we was married. She told me that she was kidnapped by a old boyfriend of hers. We talk for two weeks as well as writing each other and then I never heard from her again.

I went for a check up to see the doctor about the surgery I had. He also wanted to see me for a check up to be sure that I was in good health.

While I'm in medical for my check up, I started having a conversation with one of my Christian brother's (J). While J and I are having a conversation, a inmate is sitting down near J and I This inmate is pilling paint off the wall with his hands, For what reason I don't know. The the inmate that has been pilling paint off the wall was called In ahead of J and I to be seen by the doctor. When the doctor is finish with him. The inmate leave's and go back to his dorm. A female officer comes out of the officer station and blame J and I for the paint that was pilled off the wall. J and I see the doctor and heads back to the dorm that we are in. As soon as we get inside the dorm, J name is called along with my name to report to the officer station. When we get to the officer station, the officer tell's J and I that we need to go back to medical. J and I had no Ideal that we was in trouble for something that we didn't do. We walk back up to medical and the female officer comes up to J and I and said, "I know you to have been pilling that paint off my wall." She looks at J and J said, "we haven't done anything like that. The officer lady said, "I don't want to hear it, then she looks at me." I look up facing the top of the door and she say, "no he is not going to help you with this, go get those supply's, you two are going to clean. I didn't say much." So J and I obeyed and started cleaning. What I didn't know was that this punishment would turn into a blessing. As we started cleaning I know that I was doing a good job because the nurse that would walk by would say things like, it hasn't been this clean in here in a while, man it sure is clean in here. As I'm cleaning, the white shirt walks in and is well please of how clean the place is looking. This makes the officer lady proud of her self. After a hour or so, she walks up to J and said, "you can go back to the dorm. She then walks up to me and said, "hey *Love Forever*, I want to thank you for cleaning up so good, do you think you would want a job up here." I said, yes ma'am, its no problem." So the next day I go up to medical to work. The lady officer also have another worker that has been working up there before I started but he hasn't been doing a good job.

I come in early before he gets in and get everything clean and looking nice. When I go take out the trash, I go around getting all of the trash cans from each nurse office. I go into this one nurse office to get the trash can but I see that the trash can doesn't need taking out. When I look closer I notice that the trash can has a clean trash bag in it with a store brought coffee cake that's still in the wrapper. I look up and the nurse is looking at me. She said, "go ahead and take it." O said, "I'm okay, because I thought to myself that this coffee cake was for the other inmate worker that's been working here long before me. The lady nurse said, no no no, go ahead and take it." I said no no no, I'm sure, I'm going to leave that for the other worker. While the nurse and I were going back and forward about the coffee cake, the other Inmate worker walks in. He just showed up for work, he takes the trash can with the coffee cake. He also heard the nurse and I conversation about the coffee cake. Little did I know that this inmate was upset with me, he didn't show it. One morning I have to go to a call out (a call out is a place other than the place you are at, like a appointment) I have a call out to classification (classification is a place where a worker tells the time left of the inmate, tells his whole sentence or talk about transfers, classification keeps up with all that information) I go up to classification for my call out and check in with the lady officer that's sitting in her station in the classification building. While I'm checking in with her I don't feel right because she give me this evil look and starts asking me questions that doesn't have anything to do with my classification appointment. She is not even the person that I'm up there to see. Little did I know, the inmate that I was working with in knew knew her well and was very good friends with her, maybe even family. She ask me while I'm standing there, She said, "who told you to work in medical." I said, "what, what are you talking about, I have permission to be working up there. She ask me more question of why I was working up there that I wasn't please with our conversation. After I saw my classification officer I left and went to work in medical. When I got in there and I greeted my boss lady (the female officer that gave me the job) I called her boss lady, the same lady that punished J and I and than given me a job) I tell my boss lady what had happened when I went to classification. My boss lady can't believe what I'm telling her (my boss lady doesn't agree with the lady in classification.

So she give her a call, she pick's up the phone and call over to classification. The evil lady pick's up the phone and I hear only little of what my boss lady is saying but what I did catch from listening to my boss, I caught the part of what she said to the evil lady, she said, if you got a problem with my worker you come through me do you understand! Then my boss lady hangs up the phone. Ten minutes later while I'm in medical cleaning the floor. The evil lady from classification comes walking in. She walks up to the officer station where my boss is sitting. My boss gets up as they began having a argument. My boss shuts the officer station door and the evil lady and my boss lady argue. Three minutes later while I'm cleaning the floor, the evil lady from classification comes out of the officer station and looks at me with a devilish smile and then laughs as she leave's medical. Five minutes later. The phone rings in the officer station. My boss picks up the phone, she then close the door to the officer station. Two minutes later she hangs up the phone and walks out the officer station. She calls my name as I walk toward her. I see tears in her eyes. When I get up closer to her, she said, "while turning her head to keep me from seeing the tears, she said, "I'm sorry *Love Forever* but you can no longer work up here and then she walks back into the officer station and close the door and put her head down. I leave and go back to the dorm.

As days and weeks pass, I notice that the dorm has become very strange and wicked. The dorm became out of order in the sight of the Lord. I would walk pass a cell that's in the dorm and I would see shameful things. I would see men laying in the bunk with another man. There would be a lot of fights and blood spilled because of the gay inmates and the inmates that would owe money to other inmates. A lot of inmates was smoking that K2 drug that was going around from the outside world. Some inmates was even dying from that stuff. That dorm had gotten so wicked, I didn't know what to do. I sure hope that I didn't have to live the rest of my time in prison, going through the motion of a wicked place. I felt like, Lot, from the bible, I felt vexed with the filthy conversation of the wicked, and seeing the out of order things that was taking place. It was a sick feeling to live around foolishness. I did the only thing that I know how to do, I prayed to the Lord.

One day while in the canteen line while buying some canteen items, suddenly out of nowhere this inmate comes up to the canteen line, he walks up, their are four inmates ahead of me and the inmate that walked up to the line starts stabbing this other inmate. It was like watching a horror movie right before your eyes. Every one moved from the canteen line as the inmate continued to stab the other inmate for a few seconds. The officers came and got the inmate that had been stab. They was in search for the other inmate that did the stabbing (ran off) They soon found him and locked him up.

I kept to myself, their was not even a hand full of peoples that I could talk to because the dorm had gotten that bad into wickedness.

One day the word gets to the warden of how bad the dorm had become. The warden comes in the dorm and tell everyone to pack their belongings. I was called to the officer station. I was told that I would be moving to a honor dorm. (The honor dorm housed inmates that didn't cause any trouble) I quickly left the officer station with joy. My other Christian brother was also moved over there with me. We was the only two, the rest of the dorm was loaded up and put on the bus to be transfer away from that prison. As I entered the honor dorm many inmates started clapping their hands in joy when I walked through the door to enter the dorm. Some of the inmates was shouting my name. There was a lot of love and peace in that dorm. I felt it the moment I walked in that dorm. I had a good bunkie, he was in the word, it was much quiet in that dorm. I gave thanks to the Lord for being in the honor dorm. Many brothers in Christ would have bible study at night. We would all get together and read the word together and pray. This dorm was truly bless of the Lord. Even the inmates that wasn't walking in the word of the Lord soon started changing their life because of the movement and vibe that was taking place in that dorm. Mr. Davis was the officer in charge of the honor dorm. He was a godly man, we would have classes and he would be one of the teachers in the class that he would hold. There was a lot of different classes through out the week doing the day time. Different people that was in the word that came from the outside world would come to the honor dorm and have class, all of the classes that I attended dealt with positive thinking.

Truly I was bless to be there, the time went by so fast. Some of the inmates that left and went home, we all would hear about them doing good on the outside, such as finding a job and a place to stay and attending church. Their was very few that, when they went home we heard about their downfall or saw them on the news. One guy went home to the money that his mother left him when she passed away and later we learned that the guy that went home from the honor dorm, went out there and got a hold of some drugs and burst his heart. He wasn't out there no longer than a week before we got the news about him.

My bunkie ended up transferring to another prison and I ended up with another bunkie. He was going through a lot of problems. The dorm that he left from, he was having trouble with the inmates over there. I said, "Field, do you know the Lord? the Lord is the only one who can get you out of your troubles with those guys over there," I also said to Field, I said, "if I was you I would get into the word man, you don't know what you are missing out on, the Lord can protect you from your troubles." Field had another religion that he was into.

As weeks passed by Field comes to me for prayer because those inmates wouldn't stop threatening him, they were trying to put pressure on him on every side. I prayed for Field, we held hands right there in the cell that we were living in and I ask the Lord to protect Field and keep him safe. When we finished praying I told Field that he could trust the only.

The next day the same thing happened, they was threatening Field. I told Field, I said, "do you still have those other religious books in your locker? Field said, "yeah." I said, "this could be the reason why they are still bothering you." I said to Field, take those books that you have that's not of the Lord Jesus Christ and throw those books away. Field did as he was told. I also told Field to get *a* King James Bible. He also found a King James Bible because there was a lot of different books in the dorm to choose from.

A week went by, the troubling inmates had not said one word to Field. Soon Field looked up and didn't see the inmates anymore, the Lord had dealt with them because Field had became closer to the Lord.

As weeks went by I talked to my mother on the phone and she told me that my sister was locked up in jail. She ended up going to prison and I was able to get permission from classification to write her at the females prison were she was housed. She only had a few months to do. I would write her and encourage her about seeking the Lord. The more I explained the word of the Lord, the more she would choose her own way. I continued to pray for her. I would also prayed for the Lord to send me someone's that I could be friends with and share the word with.

CHAPTER 16

PSALM 116 15

Precious in the sight of the Lord is
the death of his saints.

The next day I get a letter from mail call, it's a letter from my sister Nora that's in prison. As I read the letter I was surprise at the things that she was saying in the letter. She told me in the letter that she had met a friend over there where she is doing her time. She said, that she told the lady why is she always smiling. The lady said to her that it was the joy of the Lord is the reason why she smile's. Her name was Shay, Shay told her that she was in the word of God and that she refuse to let anything get in her way of her relationship with the Lord. My sister told Shay that I was also in the word of God and she thought it would be a good deed for us to become friends. As I continued reading my letter I noticed another letter that came with the envelope. There was a letter from Shay. When I was finished reading the letter from my sister. I picked up the letter that Shay had written to me. She told me her name and that she was in the word of God and that she only had one month left to do in prison. She also said that she wanted to get to know me. I knew that it was my prayer to the Lord. I felt so bless because just the other night I had prayed to the Lord to send me someone and he did. I just didn't know that it was going to be that quick.

As days went by I continued to receive a letter, one out of a week from Shay, with my sister name on the envelope.

It was always a beautiful day in the honor dorm. I decided to get me a hair cut from my Christian brother Peachie. As he cut my hair, he would talk about his plans of what he will do when he got out of prison in three months. We shared with each other the word of God. Peachie was a bless person, many inmates loved Peachie. He was very good at cutting hair. He could cut anybody hair no matter what color you were. He was a true brother in the Lord. He loved drinking his coffee. As he finished cutting my hair, I gave him some canteen food for cutting my hair. Many inmates in prison use canteen items like money because in prison, it is money, it's just money in food form. Peachie told me he was okay and he didn't need anything, with joy and with the loves of God in my heart, I sad, "don't do me like that brother, I'm greatful for what you do." He took the canteen items and I left to go to my cell.

The next morning everyone ways enjoying the day. We took classes when it was time to take classes and we went to lunch together as a dorm. The day was so beautiful it was always lovely days while living in the honor dorm. Every one got along good and if there was anyone that caused any inmates trouble, Officer Davis would see to it that he kept the peace in the dorm.

After lunch everyone in the honor dorm went back to the dorm for count time. When count time was over with, we headed outside to the rec yard. That would be our daily routine. Every one would go outside and run the track, play basketball or other games that we was allowed to have on the rec yard.

We sat in our cells waiting for count to clear. When count was cleared, most of the inmates in the honor dorm would go out side. Some of the honor dorm would go out to go to the canteen window. Nobody really was without anything, We all looked out for each other and made sure that we had If we didn't have, that's just how it was in the honor dorm. It was love, peace and joy, no troublesome cellmates to make time hard, just a blessing to do time with less worries.

Count was cleared and as the dorm started walking out from the dorm to the rec yard. I look to my left and I see Peachie walking along the side of me with a smile on his face and with that Christian glow in his eyes. That was one thing about Peachie, he had that glow about his self that everyone saw.

I said to Peachie, I said, "hey Peachie what's up man? you look like you getting ready to play some basketball? Peachie said, "yeah, I'm getting ready to play some basketball." We all headed to the rec yard, when I got out there I said a few words to Mike. I still would see Mike because he was moved to the honor dorm, but he had been over there three months before I got over there. Though Mike was in a different dorm, the honor dorm program was so bless that Officer Davis would let us go to the other honor dorm to visit others that walked the path of the Lord. Some times we would leave to visit with the other honor dorm because they may have a better movie playing than the honor dorm that I was in.

While on the rec yard, I tell Mike that I'm going to jog and that I will get up with him when I finished. As I begin to jog. I jog a few laps and as I'm jogging I could see e inmates playing basketball. I also see Peachie playing basketball. Those inmates were playing full court. I continued to jog a few more laps and as I round the corner while jogging, I would see the basketball court and the inmates that's playing basketball. As I'm jogging I look up towards the basketball court and see a commotion. I see a lot of inmates that were playing basketball standing around in a circle. One inmate is on the ground, I stop to see what was going on I look and realize that its Peachie laying on the ground I said to myself, what in the world is going on. This is the honor dorm, I know theirs nobody fighting or anything. As I get closed to Peachie who's laying on the ground on his back. I see a friend trying to help Peachie because they said that Peachie had stopped breathing. The nurse soon comes running with a medical bed with wheels on it. They put Peachie on the medical bed and then takeoff running with Peachie in the medical bed, suddenly the nurse slows down and shake her head left to right and at that moment we realize that Peachie had died. I will never forget that day. That was the most saddest day ever in the honor dorm. As we all headed back inside the dorm, 30 minutes later officer Davis comes in the honor dorm and explain to everyone that Peachie had passed away. Mr. Davis said, "let us all come together in prayer for Peachie family". We all joined hands in a circle and prayed for strength for Peachie family. Every one in the honor dorm was shaken by Peachie death. I went to my cell and looked out the window as I thought about the good times that I shared with Peachie. The whole honor dorm was very quiet. Everyone was in their own my set about the times that they shared with Peachie and how he would be greatly missed.

The next day when every one went outside, before we did anything, everyone formed a circle around the basketball court and prayed again for Peachie family. As the days and the weeks passed on, everyone in the honor dorm slowly got back into the routine of things. I met up with Mike on the rec yard and he was telling me that some inmate was bothering him. Some of the inmates hated Mike because of his charges. I would always tell Mike not to let things like that get to him because in the Lord eyes, sin is sin. I told Mike that we all have sin and that I leave all the judging to the Lord.

One day doing mail call I get a letter from Skay. She told me when I get this letter, she would be free. Shay was released from the women's prison. Before she left I would encourage her through my letters to be strong in the Lord. Shay began to like me and she would pray for the Lord to release me from prison. I had started talking to Shay on the phone when I would call my mother. My mother would call Shay for me and let us talk. Shay was having a hard time out there with finding a job. The harder it got for her to find a job, the more temptation was knocking at her door. She lived with her godmother that she had known for years.

One day I'm talking to her on the phone to help encourage her and to help her cool down from being upset. Her godmother had just passed a few weeks after she was released from prison. We would pray on the phone together, a few days later she went to her godmother funeral. Her godmother was saved and believed in the Lord. So I explained to Shay that her godmother was with the Lord As days pass, it begin to get much more harder for Shay to find a job. One day while talking to Shay on the phone. I said, "let us fast unto the Lord for a job for you." We went into a fast together. Two days later when I called my mother. My mother had told me that Shay had called her to tell me that she had got a job I was so happy for her. I gave thanks to the Lord. Soon my mother slowed down on making the calls to Shay for me. It was frustrating for us because we couldn't talk to each other like we use to. Shay had started making good money as a cook. She wrote me a letter and told me that she was going to have her cellphone turn on so she could put in for the prison service so that we could talk. We waited a month wants we pit the information in. One evening I head towards the phone and try the number to her cellphone that she had given me. I had been trying everyday for a month, but on this day the phone started ringing. When I called her cellphone, I was surprise when she picked the phone up and answered. I was thankful of the Lord

88

to hear her voice. The Lord had made away for us to talk without going through anyone. We begin having a conversation and laughing with joy and being thankful of the Lord for blessing us this way. It felt like heaven had opened up. I felt bless to be able to hear a female voice every day. Being around so many men while hearing a woman's voice will bring depression on the set of the mind from not being able to be with that woman. We would pray on the phone, one day she would pray and the next day I would pray, but I would mostly do the praying. We would talk about that course of the day. Things were going lovely for Shay and I. I would at times speak to her kids and her kids would respect our conversation. I would encourage them and they would encourage me.

CHAPTER 17

NUMBERS 32:23

But if ye will not do so, behold, ye have sinned against the Lord: and be sure your sin will find you out.

As weeks turned into months. Shay boss man started having problems with the money that was being made in the store.

One day while talking to Shay on the phone, she was explaining the situation to me about her boss man and about the money problems that he was having. Shay told me while talking on the phone with her, that her boss man had cut back some of her hours. She also said that her boss man Mr. Tim had started shortening her out of her pay. We prayed for the situation. She told me for the time being that she was going to suffer through it because she needed the money. As we talked Shay told me that she was going to stay faithful to the Lord and that she was going to stay in our relationship no matter what. Shay told me that she wasn't going anywhere and I didn't need to worry about that. She said that the Lord had sent her a godly man that she had been praying for. As days continued on while calling Shay on the phone through out the days, The pressure of the world began to take hold of her. One phone call I notice that our conversation wasn't feeling as lovely as before. Another times we began to argue on the phone when I would minister to her about the situation she would be going through. She had ended up getting laid off her job and from the looks of it Mr. Tim wasn't going to take her back anytime soon. As the pressure continued in her life, she begin to look for another job. It became hard for her to find a job as the days continued to go on by. Another day while talking to her on the phone, she sounded different. I begin to question her and my questioning and ministering turned into a argument. I got off the phone with her. I called her back the next day and she told me that she was sorry and that I was right about the word of God and I told her I'm not right but the word of the Lord is right. She told me that she had messed up and smoked some weed and that she was afraid to tell me because she felt as though I would talk bad about her. I told her that I would only tell her the truth about the word of God while dealing with the situation. She told me the reason that she smoked was because of so much pressure that she was going through. She repented on the phone in prayer to the Lord. As time passed, Shay had became very upset about not having a job. She had been putting in applications after applications and only went to a few interviews, nothing good was coming her way from seeking for a job. I told Shay that I would fast and pray about the situation. I felt that I was loosing my friend Shay. Three days went by and Shay tell's me that she have a interview and the interview Is from her dream job. (She always wanted to be a nurse). One bright sunny day, Shay goes to her interview and have to take a written test. Before the written test, Shay has to take a drug test. I call her and she tell's me that she is being interviewed and taking the written test at her dream job. She said, "hubby, I'm at my dream job and I did real good on the test." I said, "praise the Lord, I'm so happy for you." She said, "call me back baby, I think they are calling for me." I said, "okay." Three hours later I call Shay back and she is very upset. I said, "hello, baby, how did everything go? She said, "you are not going to believe what happened." I said, "What? She said, "I didn't get the job because I failed the drug test, I don't understand, I prayed for forgiveness, I wanted that job! (dang!). Shay was so upset, she had slowly started rebelling against the Lord and the word of the Lord. We would argue all the time when I would call her and than one day, She stop picking up the phone when I would call. I just knew with all my heart that this was the women that the Lord had for me, but I was wrong, two weeks earlier, I had just brought shay a ring. I was able to by her a nice ring through the compensation that I received from the suffer and long wait to be treated for my bleeding situation that I had went through. I couldn't believe that it ended like this, my heart was once broken again. I went to my cell and prayed to the Lord. I prayed for whatsoever that she was going through, I also prayed for myself that the Lord will give me strength to pull through with this break up that I just suffered through. As days continued to go by. I slowly begin to get back into the form of things from the break up that I had suffered. So many broken promises had ran through my heart like rain. Their were many inmates that I was good friends with that was released from prison with the promise that they would promise to write and keep in touch with me. They never did, I would get a letter when they was released but I never would hear from them again. Surely prison is two different worlds from the outside world. Many people are forgotten, even by there love ones. It's almost impossible to hold a relationship with a friend, some of the most loving and concern friends will faded away wants their love ones are behind these prison walls.

One evening while on count time and studying the word of the Lord. I hear this screaming behind the cell doors, this inmate sound like a train going down the tracks. He'd screamed for ten minutes and stopped. When count was clear a few people walked up to his cell door to see what was going on. Some of the inmates had a ideal of what was taking place. As I looked in his cell door. I see this inmate balled up in a ball with his eyes closed. His cell had a lot of smoke in the air. This inmate had been smoking K2 and went crazy on that stuff. Officer Davis comes in the dorm and tell him to pack his things, as he comes to and begin packing his belongings, Mr. Davis was removing that inmate and his belongings out of the honor dorm. That inmate just had messed up his stay of doing easy time. Being kicked out the honor dorm was like going into hell all over again, because being place in a regular dorm comes with all kinds of unwanted surprise. Their is a chance of getting into a fight or having things stolen that belongs to you. There is no second TV to have a different option to choose from. There is one TV for 80 or more inmates to watch, so you can imagine the daily arguments that are daily when the TV comes on. There is always a TV man in every dorm, (a TV man is a inmate that try to take control of the TV) No matter what you have in mind to watch, the TV man will kill your spirit every time. A TV man will also hide and sleep with the remote control, there is one in the dorm. Some prisons have remote control and some prisons don't allow inmates to have uses of the remote control to keep down the fighting and fussing and to keep order in the dorm.

The state of prison is never good. When there is so many love ones that's waiting for you to come home or just don't know when a family member may be released because of the troubles of prison. I can say I'm truly bless to have come from such a long way.

One day while in my cell, I received a letter from a old ex girl friend. I can't believe my eyes when I see the letter because she too had faded away from me years ago. I begin reading the letter and in the letter she explain to me that she is married and have three girls. (I said to myself if you went on with your life why are you writing me, keep on going why write me now!) Rachel and I was once madly in love with each other. It was amazing how we met. I still remember to this day. I was working in this restaurant and here she comes walking in the door we both were young and it had been a little over a year from the break up from my ex wife. I had seen all of the waitress that had come in at this restaurant so I thought. There she was walking in the restaurant. I was breathless. My heart was beating as a arrow pointing her way. At that time I was a dishwasher and all the waitress loved me because I wouldn't let them clean their plates when they would bring their plates into the dish room. I would take the plate away from them quickly so that they could quickly go back to their customers table's and receive the tip's that was left for them.

After Rachel had come in, she went right away to working, when she had enough plates that needed to be wash, she came to the dish room where I was washing dishes. She looks at me in a way that she was saying, is this the one. I looked at her and said, "I'm looking for a wife." This comment took her by surprise. She smiles at me and give me her plates of dishes and then she walks off quickly. She comes back later and we talk a little and we give each other our phone number. I call her and we make plans ro go to the beach and sit and talk and get to know each. She came to my mother house and pick me up. I met her at her car and give her a hug as we both entered her car and drove to a store to get something to eat. I also brought wine to go with us. Around this time I had started back going to the church where I took my ex wife. Rachel was a very beautiful woman. She was the most beautifully woman that I had ever seen. She had the most sexy walk I had ever seen in my life, her walk was a smooth walk, like a smooth walking cat. We got the things we needed and headed for the beach. I had my mind made up that I would take it slow with Rachel.

I wanted to walk strong in the Lord and keep the faith, but Rachel was the most sexy and beautiful temptation that I ever laid my eyes on. We both had different religion's. She believe whatever can to her mind and I believe in Jesus Christ. I would minister to her and she would agree but she would look over what she was agreeing to. The more I witness to her the more she can on to me and I unto her. We arrived at the beach and started talking while walking as we held hands. We liked most of the same things and the same music. I was crazy about her and she was crazy about me. We played around the beach. I would chase her along the beach and grab her in a hug, and than we looked into each other eyes and kissed. The kissing turned into touching, the touch turned into taking our clothes off. The taking our clothes off turned into love making right there at the beach in her car. When we finished we left because she wanted to get home early to her daughter that was a few months old. She dropped me off at my mother house before it got to dark and before I got out the car we made promises of calling each other before we went to bed. I call her and we talked for a little while before I went to sleep that night. She told me that she love me and I said the same with a good night. I felt the same way about her as she felt about me. She was a very sweet and understanding person.

The next day I met Rachel at work and when our shift was over with I rode with her. We had began to leave from work together. I continued to go to church and I knew that I should marry if I was going to be having sex with her. I felt the conviction every time I went to church and the Prophet would preach on marriage. It was so hard to flee from the temptation of this woman. I would tell her the things I learned at church and before I knew it we would be making love and she would leave me with a smile on her face feeling well please. One night I ask her would she go to church with me and she agreed. The next night she pick me up with one of her friend girls in the car, we headed to church. I really wanted her to meet the Prophet preach because I said to my self If she could hear the Prophet preach maybe she will understand the walk that I was trying to walk and would start wanting the same thing. When we got in church I was a little sadden because the Prophet didn't show up that night, but little did I know that the spirit of the Lord had blessed him to be aware of this woman that I was crazy about and whom I wanted her to walk the walk with me. The church service came to a end and we left. She dropped me off and I thanked her and her friend for coming to church with me. As the week went by and came to the day of Friday of that same week. I went to church that night. The Prophet had showed up that night and I said to my self I wish he was here when I had invited Rachel to church. The Prophet begin to preach and while he was preaching he stopped and looked right at me and pointed at me and said, "that woman you are with is unsaved. I was surprise at the wisdom and knowledge that he had of the Led. He had never met Rachel ever and Rachel had never met him. When the service had ended, I greeted the man of god and I left. The next day I was full of the spirit of the Lord and I ask Rachel was she save. She had no knowledge of what being save was and I explained to her how to get save. We stopped having sex because I was trying with all my might to walk right before the Lord. Rachel and I soon went our own ways but that was my love, My Rachel. She was a sweet woman to be with. We also had a fun relationship. I thought about her strongly as I held the letter in my hand that I just received from her, I thought of her being married, that was pain to my heart but when I think about the word of the Lord and how strong he has built me, my heart is covered with respect from knowing that she is married. As I continued to read the letter, I see that she has left her phone number for me to call her. I smile to myself and think about how good it would be to hear her voice. I also wonder why she wanted me to call her if she is married.

The next day I call my mother and tell her about the good news of hearing from a old ex girlfriend, I also ask my mother to call her for me. While my mother dial's the number the phone rings two times and Rachel pick's up. I said, "hello, hey Rachel how are you? We had a conversation for a little while and then the spirit of the Lord came on me and I said doing the conversation. I said, "if I was your husband I would be mad at you, After I say this to her, she hangs up the phone." I understand what just happened, Rachel did not want to let go even in her marriage but it was to late. Rachel had move on. I never heard from her again. My heart sadden with pain as I continued to do the time that I had been sentence to do. I go back to my cell and get on my bunk and laid down to think. (life goes on)

CHAPTER 18

ECCLESIASTES 3:5

....a time to embrace, and a time to refrain from embracing

As I laid on my buck. I begin to get depressed from my mind spending with so many thoughts. My sister Nora had been released from the woman prison four weeks ago and I haven't received a letter from her since she been out of prison. I tried to steer my thoughts to happy thoughts about the first time I met Faye I begin to wrestle with the feelings I had for her that is no longer there. I remember the time when we first met. She just showed up at my grandmother house one day (God bless my grandmother soul) from being told about me, that I was a hard working man and that I lived with my grandmother. At that time we both were young, Faye and I, She showed up and I met her, we begin talking while sitting in the front yard of my grandmother house. The conversation went lovely. We made plans the next day to spend some time together. When I met Faye, she was seven months pregnant with (Shataura) her first girl. Through the next days we had gotten to know each other more. We laughed a lot at each other and I would tell her to stop at the store while we was out riding. I would always buy her things. We stopped at this one store and I went in to get some things for me. While I was in the store I had brought a watermelon. It was a very hot summer. I got in the car from coming form the store with this big watermelon and I give it to her. I said, this is for the baby." She looks at me and laugh and smile and said, "you so silly, thank you, you are sweet." We spent a lot of time together that day laughing and having a lovely conversation and getting to know each other more and more. That was so many years ago, time goes by fast. I met Faye before I ever knew who my ex wife would be. If I could turn back the hands of time, and have the mind set that I have now. I would have married Faye along time ago. Weeks had passed by and Faye and I was on the branch of being lovers. One day while out with Faye we go out and have pizza at this pizza place not to far from where my grandmother lived. We eat our pizza and enjoyed each other dearly. The next day she comes over to my grandmother house and we go in my room and talk, before I know it my sex drive goes to dancing from the sexy way that she was looking. For some reason, Faye looked very sexy being pregnant. I grab her while we was talking in my room and held her for a minute. We kissed and one thing led to another, we had sex in my room while my grandmother was on the phone (LOL) for some reason we wanted each other bad that day. 15 minutes in to sex with her, all of a sudden, her water breaks. She rush out of my room and get in the van. I couldn't believe that happened doing sex.

Thanking about those times as I laid on my bunk, I felt more depress because I felt like I should have embraced that relationship we had but I had to let that thought go to keep the pain away.

I wake up one morning and I get the word from my Christian bother that Mike had transferred. I was a little upset because I didn't get to say goodbye to my friend. He had transferred to another prison. I thought to myself maybe the transfer was better for him because he had started getting under a lot of pressure from different inmates in his dorm. When we would have class we would met up in the class and he would tell me the troubles that he had being going through. He had been in a lot of arguments and things. They wouldn't put their hands on him because they knew that I was his friend. I said to my self, I'm going to miss my friend. (Mike was the same guy that, when I first got to Santa Rosa) He was my bunkie and other inmates were trying to start trouble with him but I put a stop to that, my heart went out to him for walking in the word of the Lord and because he had the love of God in his heart.

As months passed by, we got word from officer Davis he would be leaving and going to another job. Many inmates was sad and upset with Mr. Davis because he was one of the best officers we knew.

I am very depress at this time about a lot of things so I put in to be seen by the mental health doctor. I see her and she put me on some medication for depression. I had stop going out side and jogging. The medication she put me on took me away from this world and kept my my off being depressed. I would sleep all day and be up all night.

A new month had come and the honor dorm had come to a end. Mr. Davis had left for his new job. The other officers that work at Santa Rosa had quickly started moving everyone out the honor dorm and in to a regular dorm. Mostly every one had split up and went to different dorms. It was a depressing time. No more will their be the cloud of peace in one dorm and having the peace of hanging out with mostly all Christian brothers. Everyone had a sad or either a upset look on their face, as every one started packing their belongings. I made it back to the dorm were a lot of out of order things was taking place, but it wasn't as bad as it was before, because the warden had sent mostly everyone to another prison that use to be in that dorm.

A lot of different inmates were still smoking that K2 drug even though they heard of inmates dying from it. When someone would hear that someone had died from K2, you would hear a crazy remarks of inmates saying, that's, that stuff! I want that, I want that killer.

One day as I was playing chest with a friend, a inmate went to yelling and running while taking off all of his clothes and while he also repeated rubbing his butt on the ground. A lot *of crazy* things were taking place in a regular dorm. Someone in every other dorm was getting high off K2. I couldn't believe that a inmate would see someone die from K2 and still want to smoke it. I thought about the time when I was at century, and this inmate got so high off of K2 that he got a knife and started chasing after the whole dorm as the dorm ran in a crowd. While the dorm was running, this white guy hit his foot on something on the floor and felled. While he was on the ground from falling, the rest of the inmates continued to run. As the inmate that was high from K2 continued to run and yell and make all kinds of crazy noise's, he soon caught up with the white inmate that had fell to the ground. He then took the knife and stab this white inmate many times because when he had fell, he did not get up fast enough and it had almost coast him his life al, because someone wanted to smoke K2. Many inmates that went to the box for smoking K2. Everyone that smoked K2 always would state that they didn't remember what had happened after they had smoked. As I begin to deal with being back in a regular dorm. I met my Christian brother John.

John was a jail house lawyer. He had a life sentence and once didn't know a thing about the law or how to do any law work, but one day John had made up his mind that he wasn't going to do a life sentence that the judge had given him to do. John would wake up every morning and go down to the law library and study and search to find answers until he found the right path to learn law and how to do law work. John begin to get a lot of people that he would help with their freedom. I also got John to start working on my case. It had been years since I had someone to help me with my case. I didn't trust many people to work on my case because some inmates or jailhouse lawyers as they claim to be, would take you for your canteen money and wouldn't know a thing about law, but only the professional way that they would use their words with the law and would have everyone thinking that they know the law, but the truth of the matter is that they would be eating up all of your canteen that you gave them to do your law work while they stall you by using more professional law words to make you think that they really know what they is doing. (what a crazy world we live in) By doing so, they have played with someone freedom. There has been many fights and stabbings from inmates that was taking for their love ones hard earn money that they had received from their love ones. I myself, years ago came close to getting in to a fight for that very reason. I continued to be depressed and to sleep my days away while John fought with the courts on my behalf. At this time I had been in the cell to myself because my bunkie had transferred to another prison. (never would I have guest that my new bunkie would become my best friend to be) It was early noon when I saw Alex stand in front of the officer station from having just got off the bus. I don't really know that he will be my bunkie at this time while he walks in the dorm with five other inmates that also got off the same bus that he was on. He walks in the dorm with his bible in his hand and my faith went out toward the Lord trusting him that this guy will be my bunkie. As other inmates gathered around looking to see if they knew anyone or to see if anyone maybe entering the cell of the inmate that has a cell to his self. While they walked by, I tell one of the inmates, I said, "that's my bunkie right there." I point at Alex, sure enough Alex enters the cell that I'm living In. I give him time to unpack his belongings before I walk in to speak to him. At this time Alex doesn't even know that I'm his bunkie. As minutes pass by, I walk into the cell and see Alex laying on the concrete where the mattress should be. I walk in and I tell him my name while shaking his hand. I then said, "hey man, they didn't give you no mattress? He shakes his head and said, "no, and I said, "come on man, we got to get you a mattress." Alex follows me out to the officer station and I tell the officer that Alex just got here and he needs a mattress. The officer leaves the station and find Alex a mattress with my help. There are three or four mattress in this room where they keep extra things for inmates. I go through the mattress looking for the best one I could find for my new bunkie Alex. I soon find one that's in good shape, we go back to our cell and I help Alex with putting some of his belongings in order. When we finish, we talk and I ask Alex why is he in prison. He tell me a story about a love affair of his wife cheating on him. He told me that one day he came home and caught a man hiding in his closet. He was very angry and upset and told the man to leave his house and never come back to his house. He and his wife gets into a arguments over her foolishness. A few days go by and his wife comes walking in the house with the guy. Alex and the guy argue and the guy grabs a knife and tell Alex that he would use it on him doing the argument. Alex pulls out his gun and tell the guy to get out of his house with that knife. The guy refuse and Alex tells the guy that he only has a few minutes to put the knife down and get out of his house. The guy still refuses and continues to argue with Alex. Time was up and Alex took the shot hitting the guy in the hand. The bullet goes through the guy's hand and bruises his chest. Alex wife calls the police who then arrests Alex for defending his self. I said to Alex, I said, "if only you would have left your wife when you caught the guy in the closet you wouldn't even be in prison. Alex agrees with me and shakes his head in defeat. I then started witnessing to Alex. I would give Alex the word and he would help me come out of my depression stage. We would run the track together and cook food together and have a feast. Alex was well cared for from his family. He didn't want for anything. Some inmates envy Alex. As time went on, Alex begin to let his guards down with his walk with the Lord. Alex begin to be to friendly with the very people who envied him. Some how Alex was able to get a cellphone in prison because of his wealth, soon word begin to get around to the wrong people that Alex had a cell phone. These inmates knew that Alex was friendly and they dance over his kindness. They begin to want to use his phone sometimes to all the time. Alex begin to get frustrated. I told and warren Alex about been so friendly in prison. I told him that these people would eat you alive. Alex was a Dominican, the other inmates that envied him were Spanish, but they were his own people. Alex came up with his own plan. He brought another phone, now having two phones. He said, "*Love Forever*, I got two phones now". I saw right through the situation. I said, "no Alex they got two phones now." He said, "no trust me I can handle it." I said, "okay but it just don't feel right and look right to me." I said, "you are walking the walk of faith you shouldn't even be dealing with these guys." He said,' Love Forever I can handle it, I got this, trust me." I said, "okay." Alex would let me use the phone anytime while he was at school. He would teach G.E.D to other inmates doing the morning until the after noon. Alex helped me to build a stronger relationship with my kids when he brought the phone. I would talk to them almost every night. He wasn't worry about getting caught with the phone because most of the officers didn't care what anyone did. A day or two pass and I notice that Alex didn't have none of his phones.

I ask him about it and he said that they was keeping them for him I said, "okay, you still don't see the big picture.

One day while I was gone from the dorm and standing in the medication line to get my medication, when I got my medication I go back to the dorm. When I walk in the dorm, there was five inmates standing in the cell where Alex and I was housed. I said to myself, maybe he is just talking to his friends. I said, "that I would give him a minute or so. I waited ten minutes and the five inmates were still there. I begin to get a little angry because I didn't like nobody taking up the space in a small cell, I walked toward the cell and walked in the cell and said, "everything okay in here? before I could finish saying what I was going to say. I look at Alex and see that he is holding his head. I said, "bunkie, what's up? what happened? He said that the Spanish inmates that he thought was his friends took both of his phones and one of them punched him in the head. Two days ago before this happened, Alex had brought two knifes I was very upset, I didn't like the fact that somebody hand treated my friend this way. I said, "Alex, where are the knifes you had? what's up bro." He said that he had got rid of the two knifes a day or two. He said, Love Forever, don't worry about it." I said, "I told you, I told you, but you wouldn't listen to me." I was so upset and angry. I was upset with Alex and angry with those Spanish inmates. Alex started packing his belongings and said that he was just going to get out of the dorm. He also reminders me that he didn't want me to get into any trouble. While he was packing I was making sure that no one came in the cell to put their hands on Alex. Those inmates were a bunch of cowards. They waited until I went to get my medication before they started mistreating Alex. They was very fearful of me because they knew that Alex was my friend and they knew that had I been there, and never had left to get my meds, No one would have put their hands on my friend. Alex had let his guards down and he was now packing his things to leave the dorm Alex was refraining from embracing our friendship all because he let his guards down and let the devil play him like a drum. While Alex was packing his things, one of the Spanish guys was down by the cell but not close to the cell, he was saying crazy things to Alex. I didn't say much back because Alex had decided to leave the dorm and he didn't want me to get into any trouble. I made sure that Alex would leave in one peace, while he was getting the last of his things a friend of his came in the cell to talk to Alex This Spanish inmate was kind of caught up in the middle because he was friends with the troubled Spanish inmates as well as a friend to Alex. While he was talking to Alex, as Alex continued to pack his things, the Spanish inmate that was talking to Alex grabs Alex canteen bag with Alex food items inside the bag, he takes a few items out the bag and took Alex hundred dollar canteen bag, It was so much I wanted to do but Alex didn't even want to fight for his self. The whole situation was all messed up. I was going to fix the situation with those inmates but Alex wanted no parts of anything he just wanted to leave the dorm. The inmate left with the bag and never came back. I just shook my head in anger. Alex had what he was going to take with him. I walked him out the door and helped him carry his things. I gave all of those inmates a dirty look, but there wasn't much I could do but to keep my friend safe as I walked him out the dorm. The dorm door close behind us as we got into the hallway. I tell Alex while I'm giving him a hug. I said, "no matter where you go, you are going to have to stand up for yourself because the same situation is going to happened again, you got to be strong." Alex said, "I should have listen to you." I said, "I was trying to tell you." Alex had just came to prison, so he didn't know how to adjust to his surrounding. I had been in for years when I met Alex. I said, "to Alex, God bless you." I begin to walk back into the dorm as he quickly turned his back to me because the tears was falling. I said to myself, that maybe this is the last time I would see my friend, as I entered the dorm, I see my friends as I entered the dorm.

A month had went by and it was now 2019. There was now tablets in prison. I got up one day to check my tablet and I was surprise at the message that I just had received, it said hey my name is Laly and I am very greatful of you for keeping my brother safe, he told me to write you and to let you know that he is no longer at Santa Rosa prison. They had transferred him, he said that he will never forget about you, you also can write me to get a message to him, welcome to the family, if anything I can do for you please let me know, I am very greatful of what you did.

I responded back and said hello Laly, you don't owe me anything, I would have made sure that he was safe anyway because he is my brother in the Lord and my friend." Laly text me back and thank me again and said that if I could do anything for you please let me know. I was pleased at her kindness, it felt great to feel true words because in prison every day, its a 99% chance that you are going to be lied to, either by the officers that work at the prison or by the inmates that's doing the time, and surprisedly, even by the warden at times.

Prison for the most part, is a lie house and this is why that so many love one's from the outside world relationship becomes broken, because when a love one is lied to from his love one from the out side world, it rain's down total defeat to the one who is doing time in prison. This is very hard to handle for one who is doing time in prison.

Many people in this world has at least one love one that's in prison who they either are not concern about or don't care either way. I have studied in the word of God that those that are serving the Lord is not to forget those that's are in prison, but even than those that are serving the Lord have forgotten their love ones that's in prison. My heavenly Father speaks highly of his peoples that's in prison.

There will be a time when the Lord will judge such matters.

MATTHEW 25 31-46

When the son of man shall come in his glory, and all the holy angels with him, then shall he sit upon the throne of his glory...

41 Then shall he say also unto them on the left hand, Depart from me, ye cursed, into everlastingly fire, prepared for the
devil and his angels:
42 For I was an hungred, and ye gave
me no meat: I was thirsty, and ye gave
me no drink:
43 I was a stranger, and ye took me not
in: naked, and ye clothed me not: sick, and
in prison, and ye visited me not.
44 Then shall they also answer him, saying,
Lord, when saw we thee an hungered,
or a thirst, or a stranger, or naked, or sick,
or in anger, and did not minister unto
thee?
Then shall he answer them, saying.
Verily I say unto you, inasmuch as ye did
it not to one of the least of these, ye did
it not to me,
And these shall go away into everlasting
punishment: but the righteous into life eternal.

I have learned so much while in prison. The Lord has given me so much wisdom, and one thing is clear and I speak this to all off the brothers and sisters that are in the body of Jesus Christ.

The Lord had made himself clearly when he'd stated and gave his word about love ones that's in prison. The Lord do not want you to live out your life without your concern for his people that's in prison.

HEBREWS 13 3

Remember them that are in bonds,
as bound with them and them which
suffer adversity, as being yourselves also in
the body.

As I continued to talk to Laly as the days went by we became very good friends. I found out that Laly was a very bless person. She was very kind and sweet. I truly thanked the Lord for her and her friendship.

CHAPTER 19

PHILIPPINES 1 29

For until you it is given in the behalf
of Christ, not only to believe on him, but
also to suffer for his sake

As time continued to pass, John is still trying his hardest to work on my case, the motion is complete and have been sent to the courts, three months goes by and the motion is denied. John continued to write other motion to file in the courts.

I make a phone call to my mother and doing our conversation she gives me some unwanted news. She tell me that my brother (Plook) will be coming to Santa Rosa to work as a officer. My heart dropped, I don't know how to think. I get upset and ask my mother why is he not going back to Blackwater to work.

A year ago my brother left Blackwater prison and started driving truck. He drove trucks for a month or two and decided that he didn't like the work, he than applied to return to work again as a prison guard. So he decides to work at Santa Rosa.

My mother tell me that he tried to go back to Blackwater but they wouldn't take him back because of his health. I went to thinking to myself, I thought about the suffering that I would go through. I thought about the different people that I would have to get to know and the new officers that I would have to deal with all over again. I thought about change again, I thought about have I not been caught up in a life style of sin, I wouldn't even have to go through these troubles. No sooner than one week had passed, I was being sent to the box. One morning as I was laying on my bunk, a female office[1] came to my cell and told me that the other officer is coming to cuff me up and take me to confinement (box). No sooner then she said those words, a male officer was coming in to the dorm's door with hand cuffs. (I thought to myself, here we go again) I had told my mother on the phone to let my brother know if it was possible for him to choose another prison to work at because I had a lot going on at this prison. I had just paid John to work on my case. (this can't be happening) When I leave I know that John may not continue to work on my case because I will have and need alt of my legal paper work with me. This was crazy, at this time I felt as though my brother didn't care about my freedom because he could have choose any where else to work but he choose Santa Rosa because it was closer for him, I was hurt.

I told the lady officer as the male officer was coming toward me that my things were already packed and I knew that they would be come. The male officer took me out the dorm and I was sent to confinement. Before I was place in confinement, as I was walking passed other officers, one officer ask me, he said, "what are you going to confinement for? I said, "because my brother work here now." (many officers was good friends with some of the officers at Blackwater because Blackwater and Santa Rosa was only three minutes apart between the both prison.

The officer said, "what's your brother name? I said, "Love Forever," he said, "I know him, he's a good guy.

While waiting in the box, my friend Laly text me on my tablet and made sure that I had stamps and things so that I could get In touch with my mother and other friends, those were her words. I text her back and said, "besides the Lord and my mother, you are my only friend, everyone else had left me years ago. I thanked the Lord for Laly because she was so sweet and was very helpful in that situation. She made sure to text me every few hours of everyday to check up on me until my tablet went died. Her her husband also hoped for the best for me.

While I'm in the box for two days to myself, then I was as given a bunkie, my bunkie is in the box for other reasons than a transfer. I witnessed to him and told him that I'm in the box for a transfer. He received a D.R (a trouble report). He goes to D.R court the next day and is release back to the dorm. The next day I receive another new bunkie.

This one has a cellphone with him, its a small cellphone, one that's easy to hide, A thumbs size phone. As he comes in the cell he said, "what's up bunkie? I got a phone, I just need batteries, we are going to hang out back here with this phone. He pulls it out and show it to me. One of his friends that works in the box walk's up to the cell door because Gaz (my bunkie) had call for him through the cell door. Gaz tell him to talk to one of his friends that's in one of the dorms. The inmate that works back there comes back the next day with batteries. Gaz gets the batteries from the inmate and looks at me and say we are in luck. He attached the batteries to the phone and it works. As weeks goes by we use the phone to kill some time while we are in the box because once you are in the box, there is no TV to watch, it is very boring if you don't have a book to read, it's like going into your bathroom and closing the door and the only thing that is to be received is food that you are not going to get much of and your mail and Three showers a week, while you are there you hear noise all day and all night from the yelling and loud talking of the other inmates that are doing box time as well. I had no reason to be suffering the punishment of the box. I had did nothing wrong but when a family member works at the prison you are at, that's were they place you. They do not want any contact between you and your love one that works there.

The next day twenty officers comes in to shakedown the box. All the inmates are stripped down to their boxer's and hand cuff as the officers walk every inmate out the box and place everyone in a cage while they searched the cells. When they are done, everyone returns to there cell by the officers.

The next day I receive a D.R. The officer brings the D.R to the cell door. I haven't did anything wrong so now I had to suffer a D.R. The D.R was for writers on the wall, now I know I'm not the smartest person in the world but why would I be In the box writing on the wall. I tell the officer that I just got in this cell and the writing on the wall has been there before I entered the cell. The next day I go to D.R court. I am prayed up and I'm not worried about anything because I know that I wasn't the one that put the writing on the wall, the written isn't my hand writing nor am I in a gang.

When I get inside of D.R court, the Lord was with me. The D.R court officer looked at me and said, "how do you plea? I said, "sir, I plea no guilty." He looks at me and said, "I know that you are not guilty Mr. Love Forever, I know why you're are sitting back there, we are going to find you not guilty at this time." I said, "thank you." A officer took me back to the cell.

The next day Gaz and I was moved to another cell. He complained about the toilet not working, so that we could go to another cell to get better service. The officer took us out of that cell and place us in another cell. We got better service for the phone but two hours later Gaz gets caught with the phone by a white shirt. He received a D.R and he is placed in another cell. I received another bunkie and he also had a phone but had sent for it. His phone played movies so we watch movies while looking out the cell window to be sure that a officer didn't suddenly come in the box. As time went by while waiting on my transfer, I'm very upset, I'm back there for Thanksgiving, Christmas, and my birthday.

One day while on the phone, I explain to my bunkie the reason why I'm in the box.

When night time comes, my bunkie is watching the door while I talk to my family on the phone. Suddenly my bunkie said while I'm on the phone as he's looking out the cell door he said, "this officer that's walking up to the cell door looks just like you, is this your brother? I look up and sure enough it was Plook coming to the cell door. It has been about six years since the last time I seen him at Blackwater as he walked by doing count time in training, he hasn't seen me in years.

He stands at the door and said, "They just got you sitting back here? you should be gone already. I'm going to make some calls and see what I can do. I had suffered to long in the box, I should have only waited no more than three weeks at the most for a transfer. When he finished talking, I said, "it's good to see you bro, he shakes his head in agreement and then he walks off to do his duty that he is there for.

January 22, 2020, I'm still in the box, I missed a lot of holidays while being back there.

The next day I am finally transfer. As I enter the bus, I sit down and wail for the others to get on the bus that's also being transferred.

The bus pulls off and once again I enjoy looking out the window at freedom as cars pass by and people move out and about enjoying the life of freedom. So many years has gone by. I tell myself that I don't even know what the outside world of freedom feels like anymore, but I know it's a beautiful feeling to have, to be free.

Two hours and a half, the bus pulls up at Walton C.I. prison. A few names are called including my name. When my name is called, I realize that this is my stop. I'm given a small paper telling me what dorm I'm going to be in while the officer take the hand cuffs off my hands and search through my property. I'm sent to H dorm were I entered the dorm, then the cell. I met my new bunkie, I speak to him, he doesn't say much. I also witness to him because I notice that he has a bible on his locker. It's count time and he is standing up looking at the wall with his back turned toward me. He pulls out a lock with a sock tided to it as a weapon. He put the lock and sock back into his packet. A few minutes passes by, he pulls the lock back out of his packet, then looks at it (I think to myself, what is going on with this guy) I said, "hey man you okay? is everything okay with you? is somebody going to make trouble with you? He said, "no, I wouldn't leave you in the dark like that.

The next day I came back from the chaw hall to find that he has move to another cell. I said to myself, that was weird. I begin to think about the weird and strange things that I have been through since I been in prison. I thought about a time when I was at century, and I would speak to this inmate when I would see him, a older guy. I would witness the word to him. One day as I was walking through the dorm. I notice that this older guy was sitting in his cell looking straight ahead at the wall. I entered his cell and spoke to him, I ask him was he okay, he didn't say anything, I ask him again while looking at the chicken bones that he had around his cell. Suddenly he yells out and said while holding his head, he said, "I got to get these demons out of me, he repeated this over and over as he cried. I left the cell and went and prayed for him. There was another time when I was at Lake Butler while going through my issue of blood when a inmate that was in the next cell over from me, looks straight ahead and then before I knew it, he was yelling about the devil had got into his eye. I said, "are you okay man? At that time I was listening to some godly music on my MP3 player. I said, "do you want to listen to some of this good godly music, maybe that will help you." I gave him my headphones and he put them on his ear's. I have never seen anything like that in my life, these people were dealing with a force, a demon or demons, unclean spirits that these inmates were dealing with. I didn't have much knowledge of these matters years ago, but I knew that these two inmates were dealing with something powerful. These unclean spirits were tormenting these men. Just as it was in the days of Jesus Christ when he walked the earth and dealt with these unclean spirits one on one. I have witness for myself that the word of God is true and real. I am a true believer that people can be demon possessed just as in the days of Jesus.

MARK 5:1-8

And they came over unto the other side of the sea,
into the country of the Gadarenes.
And when he was come out of the ship, immediately
there met him out of the tombs a man with an unclean
spirit.
Who had his dwelling among the tombs and no
man could bind him, no, not with chains:
Because that he had been aften bound with
fetters and chains, and the chains had been plucked
asunder by him, and the fetters broken in pieces:
neither could any man tame him.
And always, night and day, he was in
the mountains, and in the tombs, crying,
and cutting himself with stones.
But when he saw Jesus afar off, he
ran and worshipped him,
And cried with a loud voice, and said,
what have I to do with thee, Jesus, thou
son of the most high God? I adjure thee
by God, that thou torment me not.
For he said unto him, come out of the
man, thou unclean spirit.

Two weeks goes by while in the cell to myself with no bunkie, and then it happened. I get another bunkie. He walks up to the cell that I'm in with his belongings and mattress in hand. He said, "hello, I'm Peter, they just moved me over here because the cell that I'm in, the window is broken, I am gay and I know that you are in the word and don't want a gay person in the cell with you." I didn't say much, but in the pass I know the Lord had moved any homosexual far away from me. I trusted in the Lord to do the same because through much studying, I learned that nothing good comes from this kind. For whosoever chooses this path chooses death. For the wages of sin is death but the gift of God is eternal life through Jesus Christ our Lord.

To walk this path is to walk the path of wickedness, for the word of the Lord says so. These kind of people are worthy of death because of the shamefulness and the wickedness that is done in the sight of the Lord.

ROMANS 1:26-32

For this cause God gave them up unto vile affections: for even their women did change the natural use into that which is against nature: And likewise also the men, leaving the natural use of the woman, burned in their lust one toward another: men with men working that which is unseemly, and receiving in themselves that recompence of their error which was meet.

And even as they did not like to retain God in their knowledge, God gave them over to a reprobate mind, to do
those things which are not convenient,
Being filled with all unrighteousness, fornication, wickedness, covetousness, maliciousness full of envy,
murder, debate, deceit, malignity whisperers.
Back biters, haters of God, despiteful, proud, boaster, inventors of evil things, disobedient to parents,
With out understanding, covenant breakers, without
natural affection, implacable, unmerciful:
Who knowing the judgment of God, that they which
commit such things are worthy of death, not only do
the same, but have pleasure in them that do them.

Peter continued to speak, he said, "you don't have to worry about anything because I'm only going to sleep down here, I'm going to be down at the other cell with my man." I said, "okay, but I wasn't please to be around someone that was a hater of the Lord.

As time went on, Peter still haven't moved out, but when he would speak to me he would respect me, he would act in a respectful manner which was a blessing to me because I didn't want any trouble. I didn't want to get into fight mode because of the situation.

As I was ministering to him one day. He told me that he heard a voice spoke to him when he was in another dorm. He said that he was smoking and getting high and performing homosexual acts, and one night while he was sleeping he heard a voice that woke him up. The voice said it's time to put away childish things." He said that the voice scared him and that every time that he tried to sleep, the voice would speak to him by repeating, it's time to put away childish things. I told him that this was the voice of the Lord and that he should take heed to it because even I know that the Lord cares for all people and anyone can change if they choose. It's not the Father's will that anyone should perish, not even my bunkie Peter.

PETER 3 9

The Lord is not slack concerning his promise, as some men count slackness but is longsuffering to us ward, not
willing that any should perish, but that
all should come to repentance.

It is not for me to judge my bunkie (Peter) but for me to only speak the truth to him, this is what I think to myself while listening to Peter as he continued to explained of what he went through.

While he begin to talk he explain to me that out of 85% of inmates that live in the dorm, he said that only five wasn't gay including myself, I thought to myself, I said my God, this hold dorm deals in wickedness. I can't believe that I was sent to a prison like this, this could have been avoided if only my brother would have went to another prison to work. I was greatly upset and everywhere I looked around I saw a homosexual in that dorm. They were being transfer there. When I would speak to someone, my bunkie would inform me that this person or that person was gay. It was so many gay inmates there, my very soul was troubled by the situation.

The next few weeks goes by and I still have Peter as a bunkie only doing count time and when all the cell were locked for the night. Sometimes Peter would pay someone to sleep on he's bunk at night so that he could sleep with he's gay friend all night to do shameful things in the sight of the Lord.

One day while laying on my bunk and reading my bible doing count time, as soon as count was cleared and the cell doors were opened, Peter's sexmate (Lou) comes inside the cell and starts arguing with Peter. I kept on reading and while reading I hear Lou state that he would beat Peter up and at he would do something to me if I didn't keep a eye on Peter. (I thought to my self, surely this guy isn't talking to me because I don't know him and he don't know me but surely this guy was talking to me because he repeated his words. I said, "what you say? While becoming angry and upset and thinking to myself at the same time saying Lord, I'm minding my own business, how could this be happening to me. Much as I try to live daily to avoid situations, then and there, a situations had presented it self. Lou said, "you heard me if you don't keep a eye on my baby, I cut him off from speaking and said, "you are not going to do anything to me! and I'm not watching or keeping a eye on nobody. That's not my job I said while standing face to face with him. He said, "okay I'll be back, we'll handle this you don't got to say nothing else." I got madder because I was caught up in a situation that I didn't ask for. I knew that it was only the enemy trying to frustrate me. I put my shoe's on and prepared to fight because I didn't know what I was getting ready to go through. I didn't know if this would be my last day on earth or anything. I wasn't afraid, because the Lord teaches us not to be, so I stud strong as I waited by the cell door for Lou to return. Two minutes later Lou comes back and I stand strong looking him in the eye with the love of Jesus Christ but with the courage that the Lord has given me. When Lou look in my eyes he soften his approach and begin to explain his self. I said to myself while he was explaining his self, I was thinking, I thought this guy was ready for a show down, he was doing to much talking and explaining. So I listen and he left with Peter but Lou cellmate/bunkie came in the cell to talk to me on Lou behalf. His name was Chris, Chris said as he came into the cell, he said, hey man I know you be in the word and everything, I know that you keep to yourself and don't bother no one, but don't worry about Lou, he wanted me to come down here because he couldn't be a man to tell you himself that he was sorry, he told me to tell you, he's crazy in love with Peter, don't worry about him." I said, "I'm not worried, but that guy is on some foolishness, it's none of my business what he do, I don't have nothing to do with his life, I don't know why he put me in it." Chris said, "don't worry about him just pray for him." I was surprise to hear this guy speak those words because he was gay as well as Peter, that whole cell was gay, the cell were Lou was housed. I knew that I should have been praising the Lord for that trial that I went through but living in prison things become very hard most of the time, trouble will find you no matter if you are hiding in your cell all day or keeping the lowest profile. As a Christian I do know that I must suffer through trails.

CHAPTER 20

PETER 4 12-15

Beloved, think it not strange concerning the
fiery trial which is to try you, as
though some strange thing happened
unto you:
But rejoice, inasmuch as ye are partakes of
Christ's sufferings that, when
his glory shall be revealed, ye may be glad
also with exceeding joy.
If ye be reproached for, the name of
Christ, happy are ye for the spirit of glory
and of God resteth upon you: on their
part he is evil spoken of, but on your part
he is glorified.

Surely the spirit of the Lord was upon me because it was some strange things that were taking place in my life while I was at Walton prison. I took the suffer and walked through with faith in the Lord.

I didn't have anymore trouble out of Lou, in fact he was aiming to be my friend.

As time continued I walked around in the dorm listening to godly music. I see a older man in a cell as I stop to look, he is off to himself, I see that he is very humbled, so I stop and get into a godly conversation with him. I shared the word of the Lord with him and every since, he has been on fire for the Lord, he is my friend and family and brother in the Lord

(James Carroll) He was someone that I could talk to while I waited and suffered through this prison time. Nobody knows what tomorrow may bring, every day, living in prison, things became different or a change came about but nothing stayed the same. Mr. Carroll, who I call pop, he and I became very good friends. The Lord had bless me to help Mr. Carroll because nobody in his family would even support him while in prison. Mr. Carroll explain to me how he left his bank card with his son to support him while he would be in prison but his son never sent Mr. Carroll anything, My heart went out to Pop.

The more Pop begin to study the word of God and cry out to the Lord, I would see the love of God in his eyes. Mr. Carroll had that powerful glow in his eyes that everyone could easily see. I truly thanked the Lord for him. Though he and I was in the same dorm together and suffered through the shameful acts of a new day of Sodom and Gomorrah, We had our joyful times together with the peace of the Lord in the mist.

One day pop had me crying laughing, he once told me how he had broken both of his ankles. Pop explained to me that when he was on the outsides world, a long time ago he would sometimes catch a train ride home. He would jump the train. Pop explained while trying to get home one day he jump on the train and caught a ride, that day the train was moving a little to fast. He said, "when I jump off I broke the both of my ankles, my ankles had turned inward when they had broken. I said, "what did you do Pop? he said, "I just laid there and reached in my pocket, pulled out my cellphone and called for help while I was laying there, we both laughed. Pop has a way of saying things that could make you laugh with joy, love and peace but until you cry laughing.

As weeks continued to pass, I notice that this prison begin to take on a lot of problem. One of the problem was a major rate problem, these things was so big that you would think that a baby cat had ran across the cell door through out the day, some of the inmates was so afraid of them that they would almost break their neck trying to get away from those things. Some of those rates would take food from someone else cell and bring the food to another cell. These things would get a hold of anything that they may find.

Inmates that slept at the bottom bunk would wake up with a rate running form their bunk. Sometimes you could also find that these rates have reached to the top bunk as well, doing the night some inmates would try and catch them and make a pet out them. Everyday a rate or two was being killed, there were so many, these rates were getting out of control. They had started showing up more in the day time as well as night time. They would fight in the middle of the night and the noise would get so loud that it was hard to sleep a lot of times. Many inmates complained to the warden many times. Weeks and months would go by before anything was done. The complaints were so heavy by this time that the Warden had to do something because they too had started seeing with their own eyes. Soon something was done because a lot of inmates canteen were being eating away. As days went by, we all begin to see these big dead smelly rates everywhere and slowly but surely the rates went away. I was very greatful for that. The next week the grains in the shower starts being flooded with bad water that left a very bad smell. This went on for almost to weeks. Inmates that was doing box (confinement) time couldn't take a shower, it was bad. The Warden had planned, that if he couldn't got it fix that he would order everyone to be transferred out of there. The right people was called in and it took them all day to fix the problem. Professionals had to be called in to get the job done.

Three weeks after, a well had collapse in the county of Walton, the drinking water and the shower water in the prison had turned brown, no one was allowed to drink the water or shower in it, I had never seen so many things go wrong and out of order at a prison.

There was nothing pretty about the color of the buildings at Walton. The dark gray buildings would at times put inmates in a set of mind of depression. {I would say to my self, there is so much crazy things in prison that I refuse to go to hell} I refuse to go through hell on earth and than die and have to go to hell, I rather hold on to my faith in the Lord.

Doing the serving of the meal's we were given bottle water to hold us over until the problem was fix.

Two days later everything begin to fall back in place, the water was fix but we all had to let the water run so that it would clear up.

One evening Mr. Carroll was beginning to have trouble with his bunkie. Pop explain to me that every time that he would read the word, his troubled bunkie would yell and scream when he would read his bible. This was very frustrating for Mr. Carroll, it became to the point where he could not read or sleep because the troubled man would either slam the lockers while he was trying to sleep or yell and make loud noise's when he would be trying to study the word of God. I told Pop that I would talk to this man. I walk up to him and talk with him in meekness, there was something very evil about this man. After I talk with him I left the cell and went into prayer because I felt in my spirit that this troubled man would not stop being evil towards Pop.

The next day, Pop told me that some inmates from the dorm that he didn't know had spoken with the troubled man. He also told me that they had threatened the troubled man. The troubled man slowed down a little but would start back up from time to time. I told Pop to suffer through it and keep praying because the Lord knows what he is doing. I told Pop that a blessing would come if he didn't give into the foolishness that the troubled man was causing (if he didn't get angry and hurt the troubled man).

One morning the troubled man was starting up again but the Lord had moved Pop out of that dorm and place him in a bless dorm.

The dorm was a honor dorm, but it was for a lot of older inmates who had been in the service. I would see Pop walking in the chaw hall from time to time because he was in a different dorm, we would speak to each other when we could. Pop would still have that glow about himself, the glow of the Lord.

CHAPTER 21

JOHN 15:18

If the world hate you, ye know that
it hated me before it hated you

It was March 20/21, there was this bad cold going around in the dorm, many inmates was catching this cold. Many inmates was heeding to the officer station for medication to help but the meds wasn't helping. The nurse soon came and checked everyone temp, most of the inmates temps were high, so the nurse started handing out masks before we realized what covid 19 was. I felt bad, I was very cold when it was hot but yet I would be laying on my bunk under the blanket while sweating. Every one soon started finding out from the news that a out break had taken place and that everyone was getting sick, some people was dying from what the news were showing.

While in prison and suffering through these things, the only thing that would come to my mind was my passed sin, had I not been caught up in a life style of sin, I wouldn't even be in prison. I gave thanks to the Lord because I knew from much studying, that hell is much worse than being in prison, though hell is described as a prison. The only difference is that hell prison comes with fire.

Through much studying I have learned that hell has bars just as prison, there is also gates, just like prison, and there are also keys, but the only person that hold's this key is the Lord Jesus Christ.

(bars) JONAH 2:6 I went down to the bottoms of the mountains the earth with her bars was about me for ever:

(gates) MATTHEW 16:18 And I say also unto thee, that thou art Peter, and upon this rock I will build my church and the gates of hell shall not prevail against it

(keys) REVELATION 1:18 I am he that liveth, and was dead and, behold, I am alive for evermore, Amen and have the keys of hell and death

I gave thanks to the Lord, though I'm in prison, when I die, I don't have to suffer a prison hell.

While weeks passed I became better again, I recovered from being sick from covid 19, that was a blessing from the Lord.

I get word through another inmate that Mr. Carroll had transferred to another prison, it was also told to me that Mr. Carroll had been transferred to Jefferson prison. My heart went out to my friend, my brother in Christ. I was sadden to know that he was gone but I was glad that he had went to another prison other than this one. A place of wickedness. The officers were very mean at this prison. They were very hateful. They came to work hateful and left work hateful. I couldn't understand it, it's like they didn't enjoy the outside word.

One day doing inspection, (inspection is when the Warden and the Warden to be, comes in the dorm to make sure that the inmates kept their cell clean as well as the dorm) Doing this day, the Warden was coming through the dorm for inspection. He stop at my cell and step in and look at me, then he said, "get those wrinkles out of your pillowcase. It was impossible for the wrinkles to come out of my pillowcase, I tried the best way that I could. Suddenly he becomes angry and said, "do you know who I am! I'm the Warden, he said this while hitting his chest. I shook my head as I looked at the ground. The Warden told one of his officers to put handcuffs on me, and said, "lock him up! I said, "for what Sir, I didn't do anything." The Warden looks at his officer and said, "will find something to lock him up for." (I thought to myself, I said this is crazy) I later found out that the Warden wasn't please with me for writing a report on him to a higher up. So this was his way of retaliating against me. I spent a month in the box with no D.R (a report of why I was in the box) I was let out the box and I was place in another cell. Peter had transferred to another prison. I had a new bunkie name Jarome, his leg's were messed up from a stroke that he had years ago. I tried to be as much help to him as I could, because it was hard on his leg's to make his bunk up. I would make it up for him for free because he would pay other inmates to make it up for him at times. I begin to have a conversation with Jerome and witness to him. Jerome had been to prison seven times. I asked him was he tired of being in prison and when he got out this time would he allow his self to come back. He said that when he got released that he wasn't coming back. Some where in his life time he had believed in the Lord but had given up on him. I would have to put him on his bunk a lot because he would get high everyday and every time that he got high he would pass out and go to sleep and wake up a hour later and do the same thing all over again. He would also sell his food off off his tray to get high everyday.

One day he came in with a bad cold and we both got sick, we had covid, this was my second time catching it. The nurse checked our temp and saw that it was high indeed. We was place in the box in a two man cell away from the dorm that we was in to keep others from catching covid 19.

We stayed in the box for 14 days, doing the 14 days, I was sick as a dog and I felt close to death, my legs gave out one night while heading for the toilet to use the bathroom. I laid on the floor and closed my eyes as my head begin to spend and as I felt as though I was standing on the outside of my body looking at myself. I laid there and prayed and the Lord gave me strength to get on my bunk. I couldn't taste anything nor smell anything. I was messed up. I would listen to the news and listen to Tony Eveans preach on the radio. I ask my bunkie Jarome one night, I said, "when we get out of here are you going to continue to smoke that stuff." He said, "no I'm done with that stuff, I'm not smoking no more." I said, "okay, you just saying that now. I would share my canteen with Jerome. But I later found out that he would go and give it away so that he could get high, so when I would give him things to eat I would open up the food of whatever it maybe, a soup, cookies, any food items because most of the inmates didn't want anything that was open so that put a stop to him trading my canteen for drugs. I learned through studying the word of God that a double minded man is unstable in all his ways James 1:8

When our 14 days were over, our temp was gone away and we returned back to our cell.

I caught a D.R for letting my mother do a three way call for two inmates so they could talk to their family doing these trouble times that the Lord spoke of.

MATTHEW 24:7-8

For nation shall rise against nation, and kingdom against kingdom and there shall be famines, and pestilences, and earthquakes, in diver places.

All these are the beginning of sorrows.

I received my D.R through mail call and the punishment that I received was for the phone to be suspended for 30 days. I was guilty so I took what I put out. This prison had no A/C, no cooling air, I begin to complained to my mental health doctor. I told her that the meds was working against me and because it was to hot inside the dorm. I later found a case were a inmate had died in the cell, because of the medication and the heat didn't mix. Some mental health meds are not to be taken while in the heat or around any heat. I didn't know at the time that my mental health doctor was working on a transfer for me to be transferred away from that evil hot in the summer time prison.

As months went by nothing was done. I was still going through the suffering of that prison of wickedness and being hot and dealing with the hate of the officers. I watch stabbing take place while I was there. I seen men beat up their lovers of other men. (I thought to myself, surely Lord, this can't be life, this can't be how I do the rest of my time everyday, this is to much)

One day I call my mother and she told me that my aunt had passed. Laly also kept in touch with me and felt my pain as my aunt passed. She had passed from covid.

Three weeks later, another one of my aunt's had passed away. That covid were killing people left to right. Surely this was a time of sorry. I believe with all my heart that the covid was here because of the sins of the world. Many people has forgotten about the Lord, only if we all would repent, then the Lord will heal the land, only if we all would turn to the Lord.

One day while still at Walton, one of my old bunkies that was only my bunkie for a few days was very troubled, he was the most cursing man I every seen. His radio needed fixing and I fixed it for him but every time I turned around he would always want this or that done to his radio. It became overwhelming, next came his anger, I saw it coming, he would try to argue with me about the smallest things. One night, I had enough of being nice to him and showing godly love, only to be rejected and receive hate. While coming in the cell one night, he started a argument with me because I didn't tell him what he thought that I should have told him, Buster got up in my face in a fighting stand while yelling and fussing at me. I walked off to keep from hurting him and getting into trouble my aim was and still is, to please the Lord. I got on the phone to call my mother. She picked up the phone quickly that day and I told her of what was going on. I ask her if she would call the prison that I'm at and ask the captain could he move me to another cell because of the trouble that my bunkie was causing me. Before I could get off the phone, I was placed in another cell. I was very greatful of the Lord, and that is how Jerome became my bunkie. (This took place before Peter was my bunkie, Buster was my bunkie for only a few days. While doing time and having Jerome for a bunkie, Jerome continued to get high and would pass out more and more. I begin to get tired of helping him because he didn't care about helping his self. I begin to slow down on helping him. I told him one day, I said, "if you could go out and get high you can make your bunk and put your own self on the bunk." I said, "if you have a problem getting in the bunk when you get high than maybe you need to stop getting high.

While I'm suffering from trying to help Jerome and dealing with his out of order action, one evening as I walked through the dorm I see Buster talking to one of his friends, Buster was in great pain, he was crying like a new born baby. I later found out that his twin sister had pass, someone had shot her. Later that day he ask to speak to me. Even though we had our issue I was always willing to forgive and talk and listen and help in any way. Buster enter my cell and tell me that he is sorry. He said, "some times I act crazy and I know that I be in the wrong." I said, "don't worry about it, you are forgiven bro." He was in tears from the lost of his twin sister. When she died, she had left her little girl behind.

I told Buster that he need to do what's right so that he could be out there with his sister daughter. I said, "she is going to need you." I finished the conversation with ministering to him and letting him know that if he need anything that I'm here, he left.

The next day I was upset with Jerome, every time I looked around he was smoking with his friends in the cell that I slept in. Every time I left the cell they would enter the cell and fill it up with smoke, I hated the very smell of it. The Lord had delivered me from the very thought of smoke. I go in the cell when everyone leaves and I tell Jerome that there will be no more smoking in this cell, I will not put up with it, He agrees with me because I was the one that was helping him get to his bunk and make his bunk up, but even that was soon put to a stop. The next day while listening to Tony Eveans on my radio, Buster comes in, I really didn't want to have no dealing with him because he was still living a unsave and wicked life. When his sister passed he had gotten worse. He had gotten more evil with his words and actions. Buster said, "hey brother Love Forever, could you look at my radio for me" I said, "not right now, it will be later I said this while trying to listen to Tony Eveans preaching. He continued to talk about me fixing his radio. I begin to tell him that I need to look and check and see if I still have my tools to fix it with. I said, "since I moved out of the cell with you I haven't been able to fix on radio's because it put me to close to the dorms door and I don't really want to take a chance of loosing any of my tools." He begin to get angry and said, "I should break your radio." He repeated saying those words. I said, "brother if you break my radio, I won't be worry because it's not mine radio, its the Lord's. So if you break it the Lord will give me another one. Suddenly while I'm sitting on the top bunk with my head and back sitting up on the wall, he reaches up and snatched my radio in a quick motion and throw it on the ground and stomp on it. I look at my radio and with quick motion I jump down off from the top bunk and he runs out of the cell. I am very angry, not only angry because he broke my radio, but angry because I was listening to the word of God. I was listening to Tony Eveans preach the word of the Lord. So while on the floor picking up the pieces, I have had it with this guy. I put my shoe's on and I tell myself, if he even just walks pass me I'm going to beat understanding into his head. I did everything in my might to show love to this guy and yet in return he gave me hate, no matter how many times I would forgive him, he would still find a way to trouble me. I said to myself, this was the last time that I would allow this guy to disrespect me. Buster stud in his cell door not saying a word. He knew that I wasn't playing no more kindness out of my heart games with him. As the days passed, the Lord had blessed me with another radio, a greater radio. So I begin to let things go but I still kept my guard's up whenever Buster was around because I refuse to let this guy troubled me any longer. When he would see me, he would go the other way. I thank the Lord for that, one of my Christian brothers would talk to him from time to time and minister to him. (My friend Tony). Tony would tell me all the time that he would tell Buster about the things that he was doing that was out of order. Buster made little changes as time passed but what matter is that he made change.

One day I had got feed up with Jerome action of everyday putting him on his bunk when he got high and passed out, sometimes he would get so high he would urinate on his self, I got tired of cleaning it up. I told Jerome no more. I said to Jerome, I said Jerome, when you are not getting high you have no problem getting into your bunk, I'm not putting you on your bunk no more because you can do it yourself if you didn't get high, when you are not getting high you get on your bunk just fine.

One day doing count time, Jerome had gotten high and slid down out of his walker chair that he would carry around to help him with his legs when walking. When he had awaken, he ask me to help him get himself on his bunk, I said not a word. I wanted to show Jerome the suffer that he put his self through when he got high, he laid on the floor all night and than urinated on the floor as I got up the next morning. Jerome soon was moved to a one man cell that I was thankful of the Lord for. I had the cell to myself and than my brother Tony moved in the cell with me which made my time a little easy. Doing time with a troubled bunkie could be very stressful and it could make time very hard to do. Tony and I was wants bunkies, long ago when I was trying to get help for my issue at the time when I was sent to Lake Butler and nothing was done at the time. Back than Tony was my bunkie for three or four days and than he had transferred, but he always being one of the best bunkies to do time with. Tony was also good with fixing radios. Fixing radios in prison would keep food in the locker because someone radio or headphones was always breaking.

One day I call my mother and told her to call the inspector to report the retaliation that I had suffered through while being at Walton, the retaliation that the Warden had cause me. I also told my mother that I had written a letter to the inspector, that week of Thursday, my mother sent me a text on my tablet and told me that I didn't have to worry about the Warden anymore because Friday was his last day. She said that he would no longer be working at Walton. I showed many inmates the text, they was very happy and greatful with joy. So many other inmates had suffered from the Warden hand as well and they also was tired of such foolishness that he was causing. As weeks went by things begin to slowly change at Walton prison, things begin to change for the better. The officers had stop treating inmates so bad and they had slowed down from talking to inmates in a hash way and started respecting inmates. Truly that was a blessing from the Lord. I was very please and felt a little better about not having to worry about what this officer or that officer would be up to when he walked in the dorm, what troubles would he start with the inmates because at Walton, when I was there that was the worse of the worse and the thing is, Walton hadn't always been a bad prison to do time at from what other inmates would tell me. I never again heard from my brother John (the jail house lawyer) the guy that was working on my case when I was at Santa Rosa, I had given up on him but I continued to trust in the Lord, One morning I was called to legal mail to pick up my legal mail that was waiting for me. As I stud in line with the other inmates, I waited my turn and than I received my legal mail. It was a letter from the innocence Project of Florida. I read the letter, it read, Dear Mr. Love Forever we hope this letter find you well. I am writing to let you know we are still working on your case. We haven't forgotten about you. Currently, your case is awaiting review by a legal intern. Thank you for being patient while we work. If you have any questions, you can write to us....

I was so please because I knew that it was the Lord doing, the Lord have not left me. My faith became a little stronger as I trusted the Lord to work this situation out (truly the Lord is good!)

CHAPTER 22

HEBREWS 11:6

But without faith it is impossible to please him: for
he that cometh to God must believe that he is, and
that he is a rewarded of them that diligently
seek him.

One day while coming from the canteen, my name was called from the officer station. I said to myself, Lord what are the troubles of this day. I go to the officer station and I am surprise when the officer told me to pack up my belonging. I was being transferred. I knew in my heart that somebody was praying for me, little did I know that it was Mr. Carroll praying strong to the Lord on my behalf. I was so happy and surprise to hear that I was being transferred from such a wicked and evil troubled place. I go back to my cell and pack my things while telling my brother Tony that I am being transferred. I told him that I didn't know where I was going, but one thing I did know was for me to be transferring was of the Lord doing because, once I had caught that phone D.R, the Warden made it very clear that I wouldn't be transferring anywhere no time soon. I had put in for a good adjustment transfer because I had done nothing wrong to be placed at Walton, it was because of my brother that I was at Walton, had he not been working at Santa Rosa prison, maybe I would have still been there. I hugged my brother Tony and I left the dorm with my belongings in my hand. When I walk up to the gate to meet the transferring officer, I didn't see any buses but only a small van with a few inmates that was being transferred with me as well, it was about fifteen of us. We got on the van and rode on. I once again enjoyed the outside look of freedom as I looked outside of the van window. A hour and 30 minutes later we was pulling up to Jefferson prison. Jefferson, had just began to turn into a incentivized institution. A new thing had began taking place, a incentivized institution was for all inmates that was not trouble makers, those that didn't get into fights and for those that didn't have stabbing, and were not part of a gang. The Lord was truly separating the sheep from the goats. I had caught a D.R before I arrived at this prison. I was no trouble maker, I walked in the love and peace of the Lord.

As we got off the van, we were search and had given our property to the officers so they may search through our belongings as well. We were told where to go and which dorm that we would be in. As I was walking to the dorm, I was very surprise at how nice and respectful the officers were at this prison where I felt blessed, I knew I was blessed. As I entered the dorm and walk up to the officer station. I looked to my right and I see a old man looking at me as I did the same. As I got closer, I realize that it's Mr. Carroll (Pop!) I was so happy, Pop lights up like a Christmas tree when he sees me and I too do the same. (truly this was the hand of God) I waive at Pop because he is behind the dorm window and we can't hear each other unless the dorm door opens up.

I entered another wing of the dorm, it was not the same wing that Pop was in, but when I come to the window of the dorm I could see pop and he could see me. Word got around to me that Pop had told the inmates in the dorm that he was waiting for me. Pop had been praying for me and they didn't understand through the days and months why Pop would continue to walk up to the dorm window and look at the entering door before you entered the wing. They would ask Pop who was he waiting on, Pop would say, I'm waiting on my brother, you will see him, he will he coming just watch. As the inmates was telling me, I was over come with the joy of the Lord because Pop is truly a bless man of God and when he left Walton, I felt a part of myself become missing.

This prison was very clean and the food was a lot better, this is where I would like to stay until the Lord set me free from prison or call me home. Their is A/c, cooling air and the officers are very nice, but I know that trials must come because I'm a Christian and most Christians that are truly Christians go through the suffering of this world.

I met Pop at the chaw hall the next day as we met up together and begin eating and caught up with the joy of the Lord and what the Lord have been doing for us and has done for us. I told Pop that I was very greatful of the Lord for the prayers to the Lord for me. for praying me away from that troubled place.

As months goes by and I'm walking to the chaw hall. Suddenly I can't believe that Mike is standing right before my eyes. We got in to a joyful conversation for a few minutes while going into the chaw hall to eat our meal. Mike told me while he was on the bus ride over here, he had ran across one of the inmates that was trying to cause him harm his first day at Santa Rosa. Mike said, "I'm so glad to see you, you want believe what I went through man, when I left Santa Rosa, I went to Okaloosa prison and you wouldn't believe it if I told you, a inmate over there followed me into the bathroom and stab me and knock me out. When I came to and got myself together, I got me a knife and went looking for the inmate but he had check his self into the box." I said, "well I'm glad that you are okay man, its good to see you." He said, "it's good to see you too." I said, "tell your wife, I said hello and by the way how is she? He said, "she is doing great, tell mama I said hello." I said, "will do." It was time to leave the chaw hall, We left and went to different dorms, before we departed from each other we hugged and said our God bless you and went on.

I pray that everyone that have read this book will now make up there mind to be done with living a life style of sin because the Lord words are forever true, if you choose sin you will reap from the sinful life style that you may have chosen. It don't matter if you got all the money in the world. Money want buy you a free card away from sin or get you into heaven, it's the word of the Lord,

MATTHEW 16:26

For what is a man profited, if he shall gain the whole world, and lose his own soul?

or what shall a man give in exchange for his soul.

The only way that your sins can be covered is through the blood shed of Jesus Christ, No one has to go to hell, we choose to go to hell by not receiving Jesus Christ as our Lord and savour. If you don't want to spend the rest of your life in hell where there is no way out, please and I mean please pray this prayer. Say Lord I know that I'm a sinner and I'm wrong for living in a life style of sin. I want you to make me right Lord in Jesus name, forgive me of all my sins I'm sorry Lord, I pray for your mercy right now. I believe that your son Jesus Christ die on the cross for my sin, save me Lord in Jesus name.

If you just prayed that prayer by faith (by trusting in the Lord) you are save, you are blessed, you belong to the Lord Jesus Christ, welcome to the family I love you God bless you

Printed in the United States
by Baker & Taylor Publisher Services